Faces
of
God

"The faces of those who serve God reflect his image."

Broadman Press
Nashville, Tennessee

Daily Devotionals Based on Biblical Personalities

Faces of God

Samuel J. Schreiner

**To
The
Friendship
Bible
Class**

All Scripture quotations
are from the *Revised Standard Version of the Bible*
unless otherwise indicated.

Dewey Decimal Classification Number: 242
Library of Congress Catalog Card Number: 69-18143
Printed in the United States of America
18. Jul 69 KSP

Contents

First Week
Meet the Apostles

Almost all we know about the disciples (apostles) of Jesus is contained in the four Gospels. Only the activities of Peter and John are recorded in the early chapters of the book of Acts. These references tell us that these two were recognized as the spokesmen for the early church, although there is no record that they were ever given any authority over the church. Once they were sent on a special mission by the church to Samaria to check up on the preaching activities of Philip. Later Peter visited Antioch where Paul rebuked him for refusing to eat with the Gentile brethren. Peter addressed his first letter (1 Peter 1:1-2) to the Jews in dispersion in Asia Minor. It is assumed that he had worked among them at some time. Paul refers to him in his letter to the church at Corinth, inferring that he was known in this church. Paul also refers to Peter, John, and James (the brother of Jesus), "who were reputed to be pillars" of the Jerusalem church. Beyond this there is no scriptural record of Peter. Second-century writers report his presence and possible martyrdom in Rome, although this is not conclusive.

John is not referred to following Pentecost except in connection with Peter—his arrest for preaching in the Temple, and his mission to Samaria. It is assumed by most Bible scholars that John the apostle and "his servant John" mentioned in Revelation 1:1 are one and the same. If so, this places John on the Isle of Patmos as an exile, and since the Revelation is addressed to seven churches in Asia, it is correct to assume that John was known in these churches in Asia. Second-century writers identify him as a possible "bishop" of Ephesus. This, too, is not conclusively established, but it seems probable, since Ephesus is one of the churches mentioned in Revelation.

Besides the martyrdom of James (the brother of John) by Herod, nothing is known about the activities of the other disciples. Tradition has them roaming the known world from India to Europe. Doubtless the early persecution recorded in chapter 11 in the Acts scattered them abroad, and because of primitive communication all records of their activities have been lost. Paul and Peter were fortunate in being associated with Luke who proved himself to be an exceptionally able historian.

Andrew

John 1:35-42; 12:20-22

One of the two who heard John speak, and followed him, was Andrew, Simon Peter's brother. He first found his brother Simon, and said to him, "We have found the Messiah" (which means Christ). He brought him to Jesus (vv. 40-42).

Unlike his brother Peter, there is no record that Andrew ever preached a sermon. Preaching was apparently not his special gift, but he was constantly bringing people to know Jesus. He may be said to be one of the first to engage in personal witnessing. He began his career as a witness by bringing his brother to Jesus. Later he found a group of Greeks who inquired about Jesus. Andrew and Philip together brought them to Jesus. When Jesus inquired about food to feed the five thousand, it was Andrew who found the lad with the five loaves and two fishes and brought him to Jesus.

When Jesus formally called him to be his disciple and to be placed in training for the work of establishing his church, he left his nets without a word and followed him.

Modern evangelism is more dependent on personal witnessing than on eloquent preaching. Only a few can fill the role of the preacher, but every disciple of the Lord is a potential witness, and Jesus' Commission to "go therefore and make disciples" is not restricted to preachers of the gospel, but it is a charge to every disciple who acknowledges Christ as Lord and Saviour.

Question for Meditation: What keeps you from bringing people to Jesus?

Prayer: Our Father, we thank you for Andrew. His talents, like those of so many of us, seem to have been limited, but his enthusiasm to witness for his Lord was unlimited. Everywhere he

looked he found people who needed to meet Jesus. Create in us
Andrew's passion for bringing lost people to the Lord. Amen.

Monday
James (the son of Zebedee)
Matthew 4:21-22; Mark 10:35-40; Acts 12:1-2

*About that time Herod the king laid violent hands upon
some who belonged to the church. He killed James the
brother of John with the sword (Acts 12:1-2).*

James was an all-out disciple. He had no reservations in his
commitment to Jesus. Jesus recognized his complete devotion,
and made him one of the inner circle of three who shared
many of Jesus' most personal experiences. He was present on
the mount of transfiguration. He was present when Jesus
raised the daughter of Jairus from the dead. And when Jesus
craved human companionship in the garden of Gethsemane
he included James in the small group.

Jesus had a special fondness for James and his brother John.
They were his cousins. Their mothers were sisters. Doubtless
he knew them from childhood. Perhaps they had gone fishing
together. Jesus must have witnessed their explosive energy
many times; therefore he gave them an affectionate nickname,
"Boanerges," meaning "sons of thunder." Their proposal to
destroy a Samaritan village which did not welcome Jesus was
an example of their typically explosive natures.

Their aspiring enthusiasm led them into one serious blunder. They visualized Jesus on the throne of David, and they
saw themselves as his most trusted ministers. They had yet to
learn that Jesus' kingdom was not to be a restored Israel, but
the kingdom of God. Jesus rebuked them gently, but their
fellow disciples "were indignant."

James's uncompromising loyalty to Christ cost him his life.
He was the first of the disciples to suffer martyrdom.

Questions for Meditation: Could you be included among those who are uncompromisingly loyal to Christ? Do you defend your Lord before scoffers?

Prayer: Our Father, we commit all that we are and have to your service. Save us from indifference and indolence, from spiritual stagnation, from feeble response to do your will. Strengthen our resolve to follow you at all costs. Amen.

Tuesday

John

Mark 1:19-20; 9:38-41; John 20:1-10; Galatians 2:9

Now Jesus did many other signs in the presence of the disciples, which are not written in this book; but these are written that you may believe that Jesus is the Christ, the Son of God, and that believing you may have life in his name (John 20:30-31).

John, like the other disciples, had difficulty at first in understanding the true nature of Jesus' ministry. He believed with his contemporaries, that when the Messiah came he would restore the throne of David. This accounts for the ill-advised request he and his brother James made that they be given the preferred seats in Jesus' kingdom. But when John finally grasped Jesus' plan for the redemption of the world, it became an all-absorbing passion of his life.

John recognized the fact that belief in Jesus as the Son of God was the cornerstone of the plan of redemption. Therefore, in writing his version of the life and teachings of Jesus he made this his central theme—"that you may believe that Jesus is the Christ."

His association with Jesus was so intimate that he absorbed not only the fundamentals of his teaching, but the importance of love as the means through which the world was to be won for the Lord. Jesus had said: "By this all men will know that you are my disciples, if you have love for one another" (John 13:35). This then became the burden of his three letters to the churches: "Beloved, let us love one another; for love is of God, and he who loves is born of God and knows God" (1 John 4:7). He added: "This commandment we have from him, that he who loves God should love his brother also" (1 John 4:21).

Questions for Meditation: What is the motivating power in your life—success? wealth? power? happiness? service to your fellowman? the kingdom of God?

Prayer: Our Father, we pray that our love for you may be matched only by our love for our fellowman. We pray that in our world of suffering, misery, and injustice we may be sensitive to the needs of our neighbors. Fill us with compassion and readiness to help them bear their burdens and so prove our love for you. Amen.

Wednesday
Levi (Matthew)
Luke 5:27-32; Matthew 9:9-12

He left everything, and rose and followed him (Luke 5:28).

Matthew, as he was affectionately called by Jesus, started his career as a disciple of the Lord with a tremendous handicap. He was a publican, frequently described as a "sinner." By profession he was a Roman tax collector, hated and despised by everyone. People were condemned even for being caught in the company of a publican (Matt. 9:11). Publicans were despised not only because they were agents of hated Rome, but because they exploited the people by collecting taxes through extortion for their own personal gain. Roman tax collectors had the best paying jobs in the community, but they were outcasts.

While Matthew does not attempt to hide his ignominious past, he carefully refrains from taking credit for the feast he arranged so that his fellow tax collectors could meet Jesus too. Luke tells us that Matthew was the host for this gala occasion. Doubtless his silence was in keeping with his great humility. He was so grateful to the Lord for accepting him in the company of his disciples, and for redeeming his sinful past, that he had to introduce his old cronies to Jesus in the hope that they too might become followers of his Lord. (Was this the occasion that aroused Zacchaeus' desire to see Jesus?)

When Jesus warned his disciples about making material things their goal in life, he told them, "You cannot serve God and mammon (Matt. 6:24). How well Matthew knew this. The record says "he left everything." It was the turning point in his life. In later years, while he was recording the teachings of Jesus in the Gospel that bears his name, he remembered that Jesus had also said: "It is easier for a camel to go through the eye of a needle than for a rich man to enter the kingdom of God." Matthew knew about that struggle too.

Questions for Meditation: What is there in your past that is incompatible with your Christian discipleship? Have you left everything to follow your Lord?

Prayer: Our Father, we are so thankful that your grace and mercy are adequate to meet all our transgressions. We come to you humbly and submissively, asking for your forgiveness. Accept us as children of yours. Amen.

Thursday
Philip
John 1:43-46; 12:20-22; 14:8-9

"Lord, show us the Father, and we shall be satisfied" (John 14:8).

The Lord has need in his service for all kinds of people. He demonstrated this graphically in the selection of his disciples. He chose them for what they might become. Some of them like Peter showed great promise. It would be hard to say what Jesus saw in Judas Iscariot. He was doubtless one of Jesus' greatest disappointments.

When Jesus selected Philip, he must have had in mind an average person who had the characteristics of the millions who would follow and call him Lord and Saviour. Philip did not understand many of the things Jesus taught. He was slow of mind. When Jesus proposed to feed the five thousand, he did not count on Jesus' power to do the seemingly impossible, although he had witnessed Jesus' power on many occasions, and so he started counting the cost and pointed out how absurd the idea was. When the Greeks came seeking Jesus, he did not know what to do, so he consulted Andrew and together they led the Greeks to Jesus. In the midst of the Last Supper, Philip was daydreaming. "Lord, show us the Father," he said to Jesus. After three years of daily association with Jesus he had failed to see God in the person of Jesus.

But Philip had one redeeming act to his credit. When he first met Jesus, he recognized in him the fulfilment of prophecy, and he hurried to tell his friend Nathanael about it. Nathanael, knowing his friend's slowness to comprehend, was not impressed by Philip's announcement and challenged his conclusion. It is doubtful that Philip had ever studied the art of "personal work," but he recognized his persuasive limitations and said very simply, "Come and see." And so Philip, slow of mind but true of heart, was one of the first to lead a friend to Jesus.

Question for Meditation: Can you put your full faith in the Lord even when there are things you do not understand?

Prayer: Our Father, we are often so slow to respond to your will that we lose the real joy of following you. Because there are some things we do not understand, we dally with the things we do know you want us to do. Help us to act on what we know, and trust you to reveal more of your truth as we need it. Amen.

Simon Peter

Mark 1:16-18; Matthew 14:28-33; 16:13-23

"You are the Christ, the Son of the living God" (*Matt 16:16*).

Peter is Christianity's most controversial figure. His impulsiveness led him into frequent blunders, but it also resulted in bursts of insight and inspiration unmatched by his contemporaries. The blackest mark Peter acquired was his denial of his Lord at the trial. Fear, bewilderment, and concern for his Master led to his undoing. Peter quickly recovered his sense of reality under Jesus' "look," and he "went out and wept bitterly."

Peter's stature as an apostle grew measurably, when in a sudden burst of inspiration he identified Jesus as the Son of God. Jesus, knowing Peter's limitations, recognized that this sudden insight did not spring from Peter's spiritual perception, but that it was revealed to him by "my Father who is in heaven."

The commission, which follows this declaration of faith in the Son of God, has been a controversial issue for two thousand years. It seems clear from the text that Jesus proposed to build his church, not on Peter personally, but on the faith which he had just confessed—faith in the Son of God. Moreover, the power "to loose" and "to forgive" was not given to Peter alone but it was bestowed upon all his disciples. (See Matt. 18:18 and John 20:23.) They were enabled to loose and forgive by proclaiming the terms under which these blessings were available. They could withhold the good news by failure to proclaim God's grace and mercy and thus "bind them in slavery to sin."

Peter's forwardness made him the spokesman for the disciples on many occasions—and later for the early church—but there is no record that he exercised any authority. On the contrary, Paul on one occasion rebuked him for a hypocritical attitude toward the Gentiles. Peter won his incomparable place in the early Christian fellowship by the quality of his devotion and the enthusiasm of his ministry.

Questions for Meditation: Can you say with Peter's assurance that Jesus is the Son of God? Why would God build his church on such a volatile person as Peter?

Prayer: Our Father, we thank you for men like Peter. Although they display weaknesses common to all flesh, nevertheless they have a staunch faith that will not retreat. Give us Peter's sure insight into your plan of redemption, and his eagerness to proclaim your grace and mercy for all mankind. Amen.

Saturday
Thomas
John 11:11-16; 20:19-29

"Let us also go, that we may die with him" (*John 11:16*).

Thomas has been maligned for two thousand years by being branded "the doubter." It is difficult to see why he should be so singled out. He was one person who wanted evidence for something he was asked to believe. But he was not alone in his questioning the resurrection of Jesus. The record tells us that the report of Jesus' resurrection by the women who went to the tomb early in the morning "seemed to them [the disciples] an idle tale" (Luke 24:11).

When the two returned from Emmaus and reported their encounter with Jesus, "they [the disciples] did not believe them" (Mark 16:12). When Jesus appeared in their midst "they were startled and frightened, and supposed that they saw a spirit" (Luke 24:37). When Jesus spoke to them and they still doubted, he showed them his hands and feet and settled the ghost idea by calling for something to eat.

The incredulity of the disciples provides the strongest evidence for the resurrection. These men were not gullible and naïve. They demanded evidence. Thomas' insistence on seeing and touching expressed the minds of all of them. They were honest men, confronted with an incredible event, and they wanted the facts established beyond a doubt. Without this they could not have roamed the world preaching a living Christ, nor could they have died for a myth.

No one, in the light of the evidence these men compiled, can now honestly question the fact of the resurrection. Jesus realized that future generations of believers would be dependent upon the witness of these men, when he put his benediction on Thomas' insistence on the evidence. "Have you believed because you have seen me?" he asked. "Blessed are those who have not seen and yet believe" (John 20:29).

Question for Meditation: What kind of evidence do you want to firm your faith in the resurrection of Jesus?

Prayer: Our Father, we are grateful that you did not leave the credibility of our Lord's resurrection to the witness of the gullible and naïve. We recognize the place and importance of honest doubt. May we always be ready to doubt our doubts when we are tempted to doubt our beliefs, and so find our way to the truth. Amen.

Second Week

Meet the Apostles' Colleagues

It is unlikely that any of the immediate colleagues of the apostles were associated with Jesus except James, his brother, and probably John Mark as a young lad. They were largely early converts. Some of them might have been among the three thousand who were added to the church on the day of Pentecost. Others, like Luke and Timothy, could have been won to the Lord by Paul on his first missionary journey.

These leaders, together with the apostles, literally created the church as such. At the beginning there was no organization, no creed, no formulated doctrine, no church officers, no rituals. The Lord had left instructions about two ordinances—baptism and communion, but there was no instruction about who should administer these, where and when.

Church officers varied greatly from church to church. Paul lists seven or eight at various times. There seems to have been considerable duplication of functions between some of them. For example, bishops, elders, and deacons seem to have had administrative functions. Some of them, in some places, carried overseer responsibilities. There seems to have been no agreed upon specifications for these offices. It is not surprising, therefore, that these differences continue to exist to this day. Similar titles but with different functions may be found among the various church groups today.

The form of organization in the church also varied greatly. In the beginning the church seemed to be strictly democratic. The members themselves decided matters of policy and activities. In time officers began to arrogate to themselves more and more authority. In the beginning all churches were autonomous and independent. Their only common bond was their faith in the Lord Jesus, and the leadership of the apostles and their colleagues.

In the beginning churches were inclined to keep their ritual and form of worship simple. Their activity consisted of "teaching, fellowship, breaking of bread, and prayer." In time, these activities were elaborated. No doubt some of the later rituals were borrowed, in part, from some of the Mosaic rituals, with which they were familiar. As the hierarchy of officials grew in numbers and status, their functions in the worship multiplied, and the rituals became more rigid and formal. This too is reflected in modern church groups.

Written and official creeds were a long time in developing. In the beginning the purpose of the letters to churches by the apostles was to prevent or correct errors which began to creep into the churches. These letters constituted the creed of the early churches. It took a century or more before some church officials undertook to set forth what they hoped would be accepted as the official church creed. On these statements there was never common agreement, and they constitute the principle differences among churches today.

These were some of the problems with which the leaders of the early churches struggled.

Sunday
Barnabas
Acts 4:36-37; 11:18-26

He [Barnabas] was a good man, full of the Holy Spirit and of faith (11:24).

Luke's description of Barnabas—"a good man, full of the Holy Spirit, and of faith," qualifies him for the confidence all his associates had in him. He was a Levite, and a native of Cyprus. He seems to have had some material resources which he used in his ministry to the churches. He sold a field and donated the proceeds to the church; he, along with Paul, supported himself and was not dependent upon the churches he served (1 Cor. 9:6).

It is likely, although there is no record of it, that he was won to the Lord by those who were driven from Jerusalem to Cyprus by the first persecution, of which Saul (afterwards called Paul) was the fanatical leader. Eventually some of the Cyprus Christians came to Antioch and founded a church there. When news of this development reached Jerusalem, they sent Barnabas to Antioch, probably because of his acquaintance with the Christians from Cyprus, to establish fellowship with the new church.

Barnabas had kept in touch with Paul after he introduced him to the apostles in Jerusalem (Acts 9:26-27), and now he went to Tarsus and brought him to Antioch where they worked together for a whole year.

It was natural for the Antioch church to be missionary-minded, seeing that it was the product of the missionary efforts of the Cyprus church. Therefore they decided to set Paul and Barnabas aside to become the first full-time missionaries. After a preliminary journey into Asia Minor where they established churches in six cities, they separated, and Barnabas continued his missionary work with John Mark.

Barnabas, whose family name was Joseph, was given his new name by the Christians in Jerusalem because it described the outstanding characteristic of this able leader—"son of encouragement."

Question for Meditation: Barnabas seems to have been a very versatile leader. In how many places in the church would you be able to be effective? List them.

Prayer: Our Father, we thank you for the insight and devotion of those who, in the formative years of the church, gave clear leadership to its purposes and mission. We pray that we may never forget that its primary mission is to proclaim the gospel of your redeeming love. To this end we commit ourselves anew. Amen.

Monday
Silas
Acts 15:22-40; 16:19-24

But Paul chose Silas and departed, being commended by the brethren to the grace of the Lord (15.40).

Silas won his spurs by his faithful service in the church in Jerusalem. When the church wanted to send a representative who would faithfully deliver its message to the church in Antioch on an extremely delicate matter, it chose Silas and Judas, "leading men among the brethren" and "themselves prophets."

There is no record that Paul and Silas had ever met prior to this mission, but Silas so impressed Paul by his bearing and his devotion to the Lord that he readily selected him to be his companion on his second preaching mission to the Gentiles.

Silas was a Greek with a Roman citizenship. His Latin name was Silvanus. While we have no record of any sermon preached by Silas, Paul makes specific reference to Silas' role as a preacher to the church at Corinth (2 Cor. 1:19). It is assumed that Silas was well acquainted in the Thessalonian church, since Paul lists him along with Timothy as coauthors of both letters to that church. Peter also commends Silvanus as "a faithful brother" and transmits messages through him to the churches in Asia.

Silas suffered many abuses and threats to his liberty and life itself. He was imprisoned with Paul at Philippi. There they spent the night together in prayer and singing of hymns. When the earthquake shook the jail and liberated the prisoners, Paul and Silas refused to flee and won the jailer and his family to Christ.

Silas' service to the Lord was inextricably entwined with Paul's. He never sought preeminence as a preacher. He was content to stand in the shadow of a great man, singularly used by the Lord to carry the good news to all the world.

Question for Meditation: Silas gave full support to Paul. Are you as fully committed to support your pastor, or are you critical of him?

Prayer: Our Father, we pray that we might have the faith of the men of old, who through persecutions, rejections, and disasters persevered and never ceased to proclaim the love of God for lost sinners. Give us a passion for the lost, a love for the unlovely, and a readiness to do what you want us to do. Amen.

Luke
Acts 16:7-12; 2 Timothy 4:1-11

"Luke alone is with me" [Paul] (*2 Tim. 4:11*).

Frequently men are better known for their avocation than for their vocation. William Carey is quoted as saying: "My work is to preach the gospel of the Lord Jesus. I make shoes for a living." Paul spent a lifetime preaching the gospel and he made tents for a living.

Luke, the evangelist and author of the Gospel that bears his name, was a physician by profession, but there is no record of any medical service he ever rendered. Doubtless he had much to do with keeping frail Paul in good health, and this in itself would be ample justification for his recognition as a physician.

But Luke is known best to us as a writer—a biographer of Jesus (The Gospel According to Luke), and a historian of the early church and Paul's missionary journeys (The Acts of the Apostles).

Luke was of Greek origin. Tradition places his home in Antioch. If so, this is doubtless where he met Paul. He may have been a convert under Paul's preaching at Antioch.

Luke joined Paul's preaching mission at Troas on his second journey. From this time on, to the end of Paul's career, Luke was never far away, and Paul took comfort in the fact that "Luke is with me."

Luke emphasizes the fact that he drew his material for his Gospel from those who "from the beginning were eyewitnesses . . . , having followed all things closely for some time past" (Luke 1:1-3). Doubtless Luke's training as a physician impelled him to be a relentless searcher for facts from original sources. Luke used his talents as a writer to witness for Christ. There is no record that he ever preached a sermon. His witness was a written ministry. He had an inexhaustible subject to write about. He had a message people needed to know. He had the words of life for here and hereafter.

Question for Meditation: If you cannot talk to people about Christ, can you write to them about him?

Prayer: Our Father, we thank you for the talents you have given us. We pray that we may never neglect them, few though they may be, in our witness for you. We know that you do not hold us accountable for talents we do not have, but that you will in no case excuse us from using the talents you have given us. Amen.

Wednesday
John Mark
Acts 12:12-25; 15:36-40; 2 Timothy 4:11

"Get Mark and bring him with you; for he is very useful in serving me" [Paul] (2 Tim. 4:11).

We have great admiration for one who, having made a blunder in his youth, outlives the opprobrium and becomes a respected and revered associate in a great cause. John Mark was such a man. He might have given up and disappeared from Christian history when Paul rejected him as an undesirable companion on his second preaching mission. We do not know all the circumstances surrounding that rejection except that Mark forsook Paul and Barnabas at Perga and returned home. Most Bible students are generous and attribute his desertion to his disagreement with Paul about carrying the gospel to the Gentiles. This was a hurdle that a forward-looking man like Peter had difficulty in overcoming.

But Mark had sterling qualities of character and did not let this episode deter him from his desire to serve the cause of Christ. He was raised in a devout home. His mother was a consecrated member of the Jerusalem church. Her home was a favorite place for church prayer meetings. There are some who place Jesus' Last Supper in her home.

Mark's first step in overcoming the black mark against him was to accompany Barnabas, his cousin, on a mission to Cyprus. Later he became attached to Peter, who refers to him as "my son" (1 Peter 5:13). It is generally agreed that Mark wrote his Gospel very largely from the memories of Peter. There is also much evidence that he wrote his Gospel primarily for the Gentile reader. This indicates that he had overcome whatever prejudice he might have had about carrying the gospel to the Gentiles.

But most important is the fact that Mark redeemed himself in the esteem and affection of Paul. He was not only forgiven by Paul, but when the veteran apostle approached the end of his career he instructed Timothy to "get Mark and bring him with you [to Rome] for he is very useful in serving me."

Let Christians today who find themselves in disagreement with some of their church leaders take note of Mark, whose loyalty refused to let him desert the cause of Christ.

Question for Meditation: Have you become lukewarm toward your church because you had a disagreement with someone in it?

Prayer: Our Father, we are glad that you do not exclude us from serving you because we have at times been unfaithful to you. Jesus, who could pray for those who nailed him to the cross, also intercedes for us and restores us in your favor when we are contrite and repentant. Forgive us our transgressions and use us in your service. Amen.

Thursday
Philip (the evangelist)
Acts 8:4-8, 26-40

Then Philip opened his mouth, and beginning with this scripture he told him the good news of Jesus (v. 35).

Many people when they commit themselves to the Lord discover talents of which they were not aware. Luke was such a man—a physician; he became a talented writer. Peter an experienced fisherman became a flaming evangelist. So also Philip. He was first selected among the seven laymen to handle the material problems of the early church. He became so involved in the mission of the church to proclaim the love of God and the salvation of sinners, through Jesus' sacrifice on the cross, that he could not keep silent. Soon he was out preaching. When the first persecution broke out Philip moved into Samaria, and soon a full-scale revival was under way. It attracted the attention of the Jerusalem church and Peter and John were sent to investigate. They were not only amazed by what they saw, but they stayed to assist by "preaching the gospel to many villages of the Samaritans" (Acts 8:25).

But this was not all.

We next find Philip interpreting the Scriptures to an Ethiopian on his way to his homeland and winning him to the Lord.

Having completed this mission, Philip traveled up the Mediterranean coast as far as Caesarea, preaching the gospel wherever he went. Upon reaching Caesarea, he made this city his headquarters. Later Paul visited him there and spent several days with him.

Philip was a committed man.

Philip's commitment to the Lord was without reservation. He dedicated his entire life to the Lord. He listened to the Holy Spirit who directed him. He went wherever the Lord led.

Questions for Meditation: Is the Holy Spirit encouraging you to expand your service to the Lord? What are you doing about it?

Prayer: Our Father, we know that when we make a full commitment of ourselves, you will open the doors of opportunity and give us the insight and wisdom to proclaim your grace and mercy to those who are in need of it. Help us to act on this assurance. Amen.

Friday
James (the brother of Jesus)
Marks 6:3; John 7:1-9; James 1:1

James, a servant of God and of the Lord Jesus Christ (James 1:1).

Like Paul, James must have looked back on his early life with great humility and remorse. He grew up in the home with Jesus, his elder brother. They played games together, went to school together, and probably slept in the same bed. He must have noticed his brother's faultless character, and his remarkable understanding of the Scriptures, with which he confounded the scholars in the Temple in Jerusalem when he was twelve years old.

And yet James saw in his brother only a deluded young man who, he thought, had visions of grandeur; who acquired some mystical powers of healing and doing other unusual feats. In a somewhat sarcastic approach James and his other brothers urged Jesus to show off his powers to larger audiences (John 7:1-9). On another occasion even Jesus' mother, accompanied by his brothers, sought to bring him home, accepting the popular belief that he was "mad."

It took Jesus' resurrection to awaken James to the true identity of his brother. Paul tells us that Jesus made a special appearance to James after his resurrection (1 Cor. 15:7). Doubting James at last acknowledged Jesus as his Lord.

James became the respected leader of the Jerusalem church. Peter deferred to him. Paul on three occasions sought his counsel and advice. He was the chairman of the first convocation of the church to discuss doctrine and policies which were destined to change the world. He, personally, wrote the decision that was reached, under the guidance of the Holy Spirit, to invite the Gentiles to respond to the gospel (Acts 15:12-21).

Tradition tells us that he spent so much time on his knees in prayer that they were calloused "like camels' knees." When he wrote his letter to the Jews "in dispersion," he did not boast of himself as the brother of Jesus, but signed himself in deep humility—"James a servant of God, and of the Lord Jesus Christ."

Question for Meditation: Have you heard the story of Jesus' sacrifice in behalf of sinners so often that it no longer seems urgent to tell others?

Prayer: Our Father, we have heard the story of your plan of redemption of the lost world through the sacrifice of the Lord Jesus on the cross so often, we are no longer stirred up about telling the lost about it. Forgive us, our Father, and do not let us become complacent and indifferent. Amen.

Saturday
Timothy
Acts 16:1-5; 2 Timothy 1:3-14

I am reminded of your sincere faith, a faith that dwelt first in your grandmother Lois and your mother Eunice and now, I am sure, dwells in you [Paul] (2 Tim. 1:5).

Every great man engaged in vast and important enterprises is in need of able, devoted, and reliable lieutenants. Such an aid was Timothy to Paul, his spiritual father.

There is every likelihood that Timothy was won to the Lord

on Paul's first visit to Lystra. On his return to Lystra, young Timothy showed such spiritual maturity that Paul recognized in him an able workman and coveted him for his projected preaching tour.

Timothy proved himself to be a reliable emissary for Paul, and for many years Paul kept in touch with the churches he had established through young Timothy. The record finds him in Thessalonica, in Philippi, in Corinth, in Ephesus, and eventually in Rome.

Paul used him to carry his letters to these scattered churches, to help in the correction of error in their teaching, to report to Paul on the state of the churches, to carry funds, and to prepare the way for Paul's arrival. Timothy performed all these duties with dispatch and effectiveness.

Most of all Timothy won the confidence and love of Paul. He called him his "true son in the Lord." He is solicitous about the reception the Corinthians might give the young man, and so he admonished: "See that you put him at ease among you, for he is doing the work of the Lord" (1 Cor. 16:10). And to the Philippians Paul wrote: "I hope . . . to send Timothy to you soon, so that I may be cheered by news of you. I have no one like him" (2:19-20).

Finally, when Paul was imprisoned in Rome and knew that his end was near, he wrote to his young lieutenant: "The time of my departure has come. . . . Do your best to come to me soon" (2 Tim. 4:6-9). In his final hours the veteran warrior needed the comfort and cheer of his devoted friend.

Question for Meditation: Timothy was pleased to be an assistant to Paul. Can you be happy doing the spadework while someone else gets the honors and the acclaim?

Third Week

Meet the Steadfast

The most valuable man in any community is not necessarily the wealthiest, nor the most intellectual, nor the most popular, nor the most powerful. The most valuable person is the one who is most reliable under all circumstances. No one is in greater demand in the labor market. Business and industry are looking for him in places of management. When churches are torn asunder by conflicting factions, it is the member who is steadfast in the Lord who holds them together.

God is partial to the steadfast. "Have you considered my servant Job," he asked, "that there is none like him on the earth, a blameless and upright man?" (Job 1:8). Caleb in his old age was able to look upon his life and say, "I wholly followed the Lord my God" (Josh. 14:8). God's promises are made to those who steadfastly obey his commandments. He promised to establish Solomon's kingdom forever "if he continued resolute in keeping his commandments and his ordinances."

Paul admonished the Corinthian church to be "steadfast, immovable, always abounding in the work of the Lord" (1 Cor. 15:58). "Be watchful, stand firm in your faith, be courageous, be strong" (1 Cor. 16:13). At the end of his career Paul himself could say, "I have fought the good fight, I have finished the race, I have kept the faith" (2 Tim. 4:7).

Sunday
Caleb
Numbers 13:25-33; 14:6-10; Joshua 14:7-12
"I wholly followed the Lord" (Josh. 14:8).

Caleb may be called the "giant-killer" of the Old Testament. He not only saw all the difficulties and obstacles which his spying companions reported, but he also saw the Lord leading his Chosen People to victory. Heavily fortified cities held no discouragement for him. Even the giant sons of Anak did not terrify him. The possession of the land God had promised Abraham was the great prize to be won.

It was, indeed, a land flowing with milk and honey, luscious fruits, bountiful grain, luxuriant grazing lands for flocks and herds, and most of all a homeland for newly freed slaves wandering in the desert. These were the rewards Caleb envisioned for his people. But the people were afraid. They listened to the fainthearted. They lacked Caleb's steadfast faith in the Lord to lead them to victory.

Forty years passed. They were still nomads in the desert. Then the command to go forward came. Only Caleb and Joshua were left of those who turned their backs on the Lord in that far-off day. Eventually there came the day when the

Promised Land was being assigned to the various tribes, and Caleb stepped forward and asked for the fortified cities, and the land inhabited by the giant sons of Anak. Forty years had not dimmed his faith in the Lord. "It may be that the Lord will be with me, and I shall drive them out," he said. He had asked for the very land whose people had struck terror in the hearts of the fainthearted.

Questions for Meditation: How confident are you of ultimate victory in the Lord's cause? How much depends on you? How much on God?

Prayer: Our Father, we pray that we may be counted among your steadfast followers. Do not let us waver between the right and the wrong, the good and the evil. Help us to face the forces of evil, confident of your blessing. Give us understanding and insight that we may always be enlisted in your causes. Amen.

Monday
Joshua
Joshua 1:1-11; 24:14-18

Choose this day whom you will serve . . . but as for me and my house, we will serve the Lord (24:15).

Of all the giant personalities in the Old Testament, none was more faithful to God than Joshua. There is not the slightest suggestion of rebellion, disobedience, or even hesitation to follow the leadership of God. He was a faithful lieutenant of Moses, and when the time came for the invasion of the Promised Land, God chose Joshua to be his leader. "Moses my servant is dead"; the Lord said, "now therefore arise, go over this Jordan, you and all this people, into the land which I am giving to them."

Joshua was well trained and experienced in his role as the new leader of Israel. He witnessed the deliverance of Israel from Pharaoh. He saw the Red Sea miracle and the destruction of Pharaoh's hosts. He was there when food and water ran out in the desert and saw God's provision of manna, and water from the rock. He joined Caleb in bringing in the minority report of the spies, and urged Israel to move into the Promised Land. He led the preliminary skirmishes of God's people with the Ammonites and the Moabites. He stood guard on the mountain while Moses was receiving God's Commandments. He was horrified by the infidelity of the people when they made the golden calf and worshiped it. He witnessed the exposition of the law from Moses' lips, and helped build the tabernacle.

God can always use men like Joshua who are faithful and steadfast. No wonder God promised Joshua "no man shall be able to stand before you all the days of your life; as I was with Moses, so I will be with you; I will not fail you or forsake you" (1:5).

Questions for Meditation: How important is a leader like Joshua in the development of a moral climate in a God-fearing nation? Would it help if we measured the candidates for President of the United States by Joshua's standard?

Prayer: Our Father, you have never forsaken your followers who have been strong and of good courage to obey your Commandments. Grant that we may never turn from steadfastly doing your will. Hold us to that course all the days of our lives. Amen.

Tuesday
Samuel
1 Samuel 3:1-19; 12:1-5

Samuel grew, and the Lord was with him and let none of his words fall to the ground. And all Israel . . . knew that Samuel was established as a prophet of the Lord (3:19).

Samuel was a king maker in Israel. He chose Saul, Israel's first king, and David, his successor. Samuel was the last to combine in one person the offices of judge, priest, and prophet. He is one of very few men in the Scriptures about whom there is recorded not one instance of wrongdoing. When he was about to turn the government of Israel over to Saul, the new king, he demanded an audit, as it were, of his administration, and the people responded: "You have not defrauded us or oppressed us or taken anything from any man's hand" (1 Sam. 12:4).

Samuel's abdication of the judgeship did not diminish either his activity or his interest in the affairs of the nation. He was the counselor of the young king, albeit his counsel was not always followed. He continued as the conscience of Israel and repeatedly called on them to renew their vows to serve the Lord. He officiated regularly in the offerings of sacrifices. He rebuilt the altars of Israel.

In the separation of the temporal responsibilities under the new king, from the spiritual which he retained, Samuel saw the waning of spiritual leadership. He rebuked Saul for his effrontery to invade the sanctuary of the tabernacle by assuming to officiate at the sacrifices. In his later years he established a "school of prophets" that there should never cease to be a prophet in Israel to call the people to serve the Lord. In his final benediction he showed his steadfastness both to his people and to the Lord: "As for me, far be it from me that I should sin against the Lord by ceasing to pray for you; and I will instruct you in the good and the right way. Only fear the Lord, and serve him faithfully with all your heart" (1 Sam. 12:23–24).

Questions for Meditation: How would you explain the downfall of Saul? Was the job too big? Did it go to his head? Did he ignore the Lord?

Prayer: Our Father, sometimes we hear your voice but we are unwilling to heed it. Help us to see that our lives will be richer and fuller when they are attuned to your will. May those about us never be in doubt about our loyalty to you. Amen.

Wednesday
Esther

Esther 3:2-5; 4:13-14; 7:3-10; 8:13

Who knows whether you have not come to the kingdom for such a time as this? (4:14).

When God's purposes are being thwarted or ignored, he prepares someone to save his people. Thus he prepared Moses through a forty-year training process to deliver his people from their Egyptian bondage. When Saul failed, he had David standing in the wings ready to take his place. When the Jews who were living in Persia were in danger of annihilation, he brought Esther to be the Queen of Persia and to save God's people.

She was not an ordinary woman, as might be expected, since God chose her for the role of savior. Besides being very beautiful she possessed poise, good judgment, and courage.

She was fully aware of the protocol of the Persian court and that her presumption to enter the king's presence without his invitation could lead to her death. Nevertheless, her sense of responsibility for her people was so great that she ventured to approach the king. "If I perish, I perish," expressed her calm decision.

Esther's qualification for the responsibility of saving her people in time of crisis was her steadfast devotion to duty, even at the risk of her life.

Questions for Meditation: To what extent do you think God prepares a leader in a national crisis to save a people who are important in his purposes? Would America qualify for such a role?

Prayer: Our Father, we know that when you call us to a task that it is important, and that you have prepared us for the assignment. Help us to rise above our selfish preferences and to heed your call, even when it is an unwelcomed summons. Amen.

Thursday

Daniel

Daniel 6:4-18

When Daniel knew that the [king's] document had been signed, . . . he got down upon his knees three times a day and prayed and gave thanks before his God, as he had done previously (v. 10).

It takes tremendous fortitude and conviction to stand before a great empire and challenge its right to violate one's conscience. Daniel was not engaged in the practice of civil disobedience. His refusal to desist from praying to his God did not impinge upon the rights, privileges, well-being, or liberties of anyone else. Prayer with Daniel, as it should be with everyone, was personal communication with his God, and was clearly outside the prerogative of a ruler to deny. Moreover, this was an edict, conceived in malice and directed at one man—Daniel. Moreover, loyalty to God takes precedence over all other loyalties. "You shall have no other Gods before me" is the First Commandment. Peter emphasized the point when he resisted the threats of the scribes: "Whether it is right in the sight of God to listen to you rather than to God, you must judge" (Acts 4:19).

Daniel did not ignore the edict for the sake of showing disrespect for it. He was continuing a practice of long standing which had nothing to do with the edict. His habitual practice of prayer was based on his steadfast faith in God. He had a well-established relationship with God which sustained him in the hour of crisis. So often men are unable to reach God in their hour of need because they have not maintained an open line to him.

Questions of Meditation: Do you think God would have rescued Daniel if he had not started praying until he was threatened? Do you pray more fervently when you are in trouble?

Prayer: Our Father, we pray for those who have responsibility for the conduct of our government. We pray that you will uphold their hands when they are right, and show them their error when they are wrong. We pray that only our loyalty to you shall transcend our devotion to our country. Amen.

Friday

Stephen
Acts 7:51-60

"Lord, do not hold this sin against them" (v. 60).

Stephen's speech before the council was hardly the kind of a speech that would make friends, or even influence people, particularly when they are bent on one's destruction. It was addressed to the same collection of people who, only a few weeks before, had condemned Jesus to be sent to the cross. Stephen understood clearly that they had the power to destroy him too.

But Stephen was a man with a mission. The record says he was "full of grace and power." There is no record that he ever met Jesus personally. He was of the new generation of leaders who experienced the power of the Holy Spirit since Pentecost. He showed himself to be well grounded in the history of Israel, and he had come to see that all this history and the prophecies of God's messengers pointed to the coming of Jesus —"the righteous one."

Someone must preach the gospel even to God's enemies. Deluded people, whether through ignorance or prejudice, stand in the threat of judgment too, and must recognize their need of a savior. No soft conciliatory words would dent their hardened hearts. Sometimes the harsh and cruel truth must be spoken by God's men.

Stephen had a passion and love for all people, even those who would stone him to death.

Questions for Meditation: Could Stephen have saved himself for many years of service to the Lord if he had been less brutal toward his judges? Would you have so advised him? Why or why not?

Prayer: Our Father, help us to know when to speak the truth without equivocation, and when to soothe the spirits of those who oppose us. May we never compromise the truth you reveal to us, but may we always show brotherly love, even to our implacable enemies, for even our Lord prayed for his enemies who nailed him to a cross. Amen.

Saturday
Mary of Bethany
John 12:1-8; Mark 14:3-9

Wherever the gospel is preached in the whole world, what she has done will be told in memory of her (Mark 14:9).

To include the story of Mary of Bethany with the steadfast heroes of the Bible may seem inappropriate at first glance. Luke identifies her as a "sinner." (Aren't we all?) All of the disciples knew her and her brother Lazarus whom Jesus raised from the dead. They had been in her home when she sat at the feet of Jesus listening to his inspiring words. Her home was Jesus' favorite retreat when he was in need of rest and relaxation. But none of the Gospel writers identify her in this dining episode by name except John. It could be that they were reluctant to associate her with this amazing act of anointing Jesus' feet with such costly ointment.

Mary braved the criticisms of those who were dining with Jesus. How mortified she must have been when her loving act drew such violent objection. She might have fled in humiliation and embarrassment had not Jesus come to her defense, commending her devotion, and pronouncing the act as a beautiful service of dedication.

It was Mary's steadfast love for her Saviour, which Jesus said would be a memorial to her throughout all time, that entitles her to a place among the steadfast. She had a feeling that her Master would not be with them long (the Gospel writers tell us he was less than a week from the cross), and she was determined to show her love on every occasion.

Question for Meditation: Jesus expressed his benediction on Mary when he said: "She has done what she could." Can Jesus say that about you?

Prayer: Our Father, we confess in humble acknowledgment that we have not always done all that we could have done in proclaiming our love for the Saviour. We have been absorbed in our selfish pursuits, or we have lacked the courage to witness when we had the opportunity. Like Mary, may we spare no effort or expense to show our devotion to you. Amen.

Meet the Builders

The building program in progress in a community or a nation is usually considered a reliable indication of the vitality of its people. The world has always tipped its hat to its builders. Building is one evidence of the constructive approach to a people's needs.

Builders have played an important role in God's evolving plan for his people. They range from the preservation of the human race in Noah's ark to the economic development of Israel's resources under Uzziah. Faithfulness to his instructions was always one of God's requirements for all his builders.

Unfortunately not all of them remained faithful. Success and power diverted their loyalties to lesser gods. Their ultimate fate was destruction and defeat. The Lord's blessings are reserved for the faithful. "If at any time I declare concerning a nation or a kingdom that I will build and plant it, and if it does evil in my sight, . . . then I will repent of the good which I had intended to do to it" (Jer. 18:9–10). The psalmist has said: "Unless the Lord builds the house, those who build it labor in vain" (127:1).

But evil men build too. They built temples to pagan gods; they built towers to perpetuate their evil power; they build palaces to glorify themselves. It was Nebuchadnezzar who boasted: "Is not this great Babylon, which I have built by my mighty power . . . for the glory of my majesty" (Dan. 4:30).

Little men also build to take revenge on those who oppose their spiteful ways. Such a builder was Haman, who built a gallows for his adversary, only to find himself hanged upon it.

Sunday
Noah
Genesis 6:12-22

By faith Noah . . . took heed and constructed an ark for the saving of his household (Heb. 11:7).

No ancient Bible story has been so thoroughly corroborated by twentieth-century archaeological excavations in the homeland of the human race, as the story of the flood. Not only do the tablets from the libraries of ancient lands recount the story with astonishing fidelity to the Bible account, but layers of water-laid sediment eight feet and more deep have been uncovered in numerous excavations from Ur to Nineveh.

"Noah found favor in the eyes of the Lord" (Gen. 6:8) and God warned him that he intended to destroy the race of man because he "was sorry that he had made man on the earth, and it grieved him to his heart" (v. 6).

God gave Noah specific instructions about the Ark—its dimensions, its structure, its functions. And "Noah did . . . all that God commanded him"—even in the face of universal ridicule.

Obedience is the first requirement God makes of his people. There is no way that he can use people who are not committed to do his will. Disobedience is one of the most common reasons for unanswered prayer. "Noah was a righteous man, blameless in his generation; Noah walked with God" (v. 9).

Questions for Meditation: How faithful to do God's will would you be if everyone you knew ridiculed you? Do you think you might decide that maybe you didn't understand God correctly?

Prayer: Our Father, we pray that we may always walk in fellowship with you, and be obedient to your instructions. May we never be diverted from following you by the lure of self-interest, nor the ridicule of others. Grant that our lives may be a hymn of praise for your goodness to us. Amen.

Monday
Abraham
Genesis 12:2-18

. . . So he built there an altar to the Lord (v. 7).

Abraham was the first towering giant in the Bible story. He was called by his contemporaries "the friend of God." He represented the highest concept of divine revelation in his day. He lived day by day in conscious communication with God. Living in a polytheistic age, his unalterable faith in one living God was a revolutionary break with his contemporaries. He was firmly convinced that he was destined to be the father of many nations. Again and again God assures him of this destiny. There is not a single instance recorded where his faith in the Lord wavered.

He was obedient to the point of preparing to sacrifice his

only son, through whom God promised to build a nation. This was God's supreme test of Abraham's faithfulness. His faithfulness to God is demonstrated by his habitual practice of building altars for the worship of God. Wherever he went his first act was to build an altar, even before he pitched his own tent.

God was never a once-in-a-while experience with Abraham. The Lord was his constant companion. Consequently, God was always responsive to Abraham's need. Unanswered prayer was no problem. Even God's delay in giving him a promised son did not disturb him as it did his wife Sarah. He lived in faith that God's promises were sure and certain.

Questions for Meditation: How sure are you that you are doing what God wants you to do? Would you bet the life of your son on it?

Prayer: Our Father, we pray that you will be our constant companion; that wherever we go you will be at our side. Forbid that we should go any place that you cannot honor with your presence. Let nothing come between us to mar this fellowship. Amen.

Tuesday

Solomon
1 Kings 5:1-14

Then Solomon said [prayed], . . . "I have built thee an exalted house, a place for thee to dwell in for ever" (1 Kings 8:12-13).

Someone has said "power corrupts, and absolute power corrupts absolutely." Solomon was a living symbol of this.

In his youth he was a God-fearing man—consecrated to the worship of the Lord, eager to know and to do God's will, and to deal kindly and justly with his people. To make the worship of Jehovah more meaningful to his people, he built the most beautiful Temple of ancient Israel.

Not only did he commit himself wholly to the Lord, but he admonished his people: "Let your heart therefore be wholly true to the Lord our God, walking in his statutes and keeping his commandments" (8:61).

But Solomon's own devotion to the Lord was short-lived. He started by making a marriage alliance with the king of Egypt. Moreover, he acquired seven hundred other wives from neighboring nations, for all of whom he built places where they could worship their gods. "His wives," the record says, "turned away his heart after other gods; and his heart was not wholly true to the Lord" (1 Kings 11:4). "So Solomon did what was evil in the sight of the Lord. . . . And the Lord was angry with Solomon, because his heart had turned away from the Lord" (vv. 6–9).

Solomon's vast empire from the Euphrates to Egypt made him arrogant and tyrannical. His numerous and elaborate building projects were constructed with forced labor. He laid heavy burdens of taxation on his people to satisfy his vanity. They lived in hovels. Starvation and oppression were their lot.

In his old age, disillusioned and defeated, he summed up his bitter experience with the pathetic conclusion that "all is vanity" (Eccl. 1:2).

Questions for Meditation: Solomon was credited with unparalleled wisdom. How do you account for the tragic end of his kingdom? What constitutes true wisdom?

Prayer: O Lord my God, hearkening to the cry and to the prayer which thy servant prays before thee this day; . . . hearken thou to the supplication of thy servant and of thy people Israel, when they pray toward this place; yea, hear thou in heaven thy dwelling place; and when thou hearest, forgive" (Solomon's prayer, 1 Kings 8:28-30). Amen.

Wednesday
Zerubbabel
Ezra 3:8-13

All the people shouted with a great shout, when they praised the Lord, because the foundation of the house of the Lord was laid (v. 11).

The Lord opens doors for his servants who want to accomplish his will, but he seldom removes all the obstacles. Witness all the obstacles Moses encountered, even though God had instructed him to lead his people out of Egypt. Is it surprising, therefore, that Zerubbabel encountered many obstacles, even though he arrived in Jerusalem with an official decree from Cyrus, the Persian king, authorizing him to rebuild the Temple of the Lord God in Jerusalem?

First, he encountered interference on the part of some of the people who occupied the land. They "discouraged the people of Judah, and made them afraid to build" (4:4). Then "they wrote an accusation against the inhabitants of Judah and Jerusalem" (v. 6). Eventually, the building was stopped.

When Darius came to the throne of Persia, a letter was directed to the new king, who found that Cyrus had, indeed, authorized the rebuilding of the house of the Lord. "Then Zerubbabel . . . arose and began to rebuild the house of God" (5:2). In the sixth year of Darius it was finished.

Zerubbabel was the grandson of the last king of Judah before the captivity. He was probably born in Babylon. He was a staunch Hebrew, zealous for the welfare of his people, but he also stood high in the counsels of the Persians. Like Daniel, he was wholly committed to the Lord. Obstacles were no discouragement to him. He relied on his conviction that God had set him to the task of rebuilding the Temple. His faith was expressed in Paul's words: "If God is for us, who is against us?" (Rom. 8:31).

Questions for Meditation: Do you think that obstacles in the way of God's work are evidence that God is not pleased? Should we pray to God asking that he remove the obstacles, or does God expect us to do it?

Prayer: Our Father, do not let obstacles deter us from doing what you want us to do. We claim your assurance that you will be with us if we turn neither to the right nor to the left, but be obedient to your will. Only make us strong and of good courage. Amen.

Thursday
Nehemiah
Nehemiah 2:5-18; 4:6-23

So we built the wall; and all the wall was joined together to half its height. For the people had a mind to work (4:6).

The book of Nehemiah should be required reading for every man who holds an office of public trust or who aspires to such an office. It sets forth Nehemiah's stern principles of conduct in public office.

In their efforts to thwart his determination to rebuild the walls of Jerusalem, his enemies contrived many abuses. First, they fattened their own back accounts by exacting exorbitant interest of their impoverished neighbors. Nehemiah condemned this practice and broke the conspiracy by personally lending these people money without interest.

Then he was charged with personal profiteering through the king's food allowance. So he refused to accept the allowance. Next he was invited into conference to discuss their differences. But Nehemiah sensed the bad repute he would suffer by consorting with the enemy, so he replied: "I am doing a great work and I cannot come down" (6:3). In other words he said, "I am too busy."

Failing in this, they spread the rumor that he was planning to make himself king. This he denied emphatically. Finally, they sought to brand him with a reputation of fear. They proposed that he seek refuge in the Temple lest someone would slay him, but he said: "Should such a man as I flee?" (v. 11).

"So the wall was finished. . . . And when all our enemies heard of it, all . . . fell greatly in their own esteem; for they perceived that this work had been accomplished with the help of our God" (Neh. 6:15–16).

Question for Meditation: Would it discourage you in doing God's work if you were personally attacked and your reputation assaulted?

Prayer: Our Father, we pray that you may be able to approve the life we live, that it may be acceptable to you, and an example to our neighbors. May no one question our loyalty to you by the things they see us doing. Teach us to witness not only with our lips but also with our lives. Amen.

Friday
Uzziah
2 Chronicles 26:1-23

He built Eloth and restored it to Judah (v. 2).

Uzziah was one of the greatest, and the last great builder in ancient Israel. He reestablished Israel's access to the Gulf of Aqaba, and built the port of Eloth which has figured so prominently in modern Israel's history. He built watchtowers on the walls of Jerusalem to strengthen its defenses. He built defensive outposts along the caravan routes from Arabia to Gaza and Egypt to protect his trade. He modernized his defensive equipment. He improved and expanded his herds and flocks, and subsidized agriculture and the vineyards. He dug wells in the desert to water his herds and irrigate his lands. His power and influence was the greatest since the days of Solomon. The record says: "His fame spread far, for he was marvelously helped, til he was strong" (v. 15). "But when he was strong," the record continues, "he grew proud, to his destruction. For he was false to the Lord his God" (v. 16).

"Pride goes before destruction" (Prov. 16:18). Uzziah had become so great in his own estimation that he thought he could do no wrong, and he trespassed upon the sacred precincts of the Temple. For this usurpation he was stricken with leprosy, so that he lived and died an outcast.

"Do not be deceived; God is not mocked" (Gal. 6:7). No one becomes so powerful, important, or good, that he can disobey God with impunity. "The end of the matter; . . . Fear God, and keep his commandments; for this is the whole duty of man" (Eccl. 12:13).

Question for Meditation: A wealthy layman once told the writer, "I am afraid to quit tithing, now that I have become wealthy. God may stop blessing me. Do you think a man's obligation to God changes when he becomes wealthy, or powerful?

Prayer: Our Father, bring success to the works of our hands in all things when we undertake to do them in your name, but do not let success sway our obedience to you. We claim your promise that we shall have good success when we do your will. Amen.

Saturday
Haman
Esther 3:1-6; 4:1-17; 7:1-10

So they hanged Haman on the gallows which he had prepared for Mordecai (7:10).

Who has not looked upon some of the injustices of life—good men suffer, and bad men go free—and prayed for a better show of justice? Selfishness, greed, and intolerance are so frequently rewarded, while goodness and right are nailed to a cross. James Russell Lowell stated it this way, "Truth forever on the scaffold, wrong forever on the throne."

As natural as this reaction is, man must be reminded that goodness is not to be put on the bargain counter where it receives promptly its rewards, and wrong its punishment. The scales of justice are seldom balanced on Saturday night.

The story of Haman is a welcome switch in the routine of injustice. Haman was a small-time politician who had wormed his way into his king's confidence and gained great authority. But he was jealous, spiteful, and corrupt. When Mordecai, the Jewish foster-father of Queen Esther, refused to bow before him, his rage knew no bounds. He resolved upon the destruction of the entire Jewish people, and as a choice bit of vengeance, he built a gallows seventy-five feet high on which he would personally hang Mordecai.

But Mordecai and the beautiful queen unmasked the treacherous Haman, and a beneficent king sent him to be hanged on the gallows he had built for Mordecai.

Righteousness is its own reward. Men like Mordecai choose to do right because it is right. Really, honest people do not choose to be honest because it is the "best policy," but because it is right to be honest. Men who live by this standard command our greatest respect. Queen Esther rose to the stature of greatness when she chose the right with a simple declaration, "If I perish, I perish."

Men like Haman do not understand such fidelity to righteousness, but they build gallows on which they sometimes perish themselves.

Questions for Meditation: Does your faith in the Lord falter when it costs you to do right, and only evil comes your way? What is the best reason you can give for doing right?

Meet the Headliners for a Day

Some men occupy the center of life's stage for just a moment in time, but in that brief instant they determine the course of history. They serve their fellowman for weal or woe and then move on. They fix their own places in history. They write their names in the book of life, or rub it out.

Some of the men we have selected who played such headline roles moved on and off the stage in a matter of days, sometimes even in hours, but they left an indelible record for posterity to read. In our American history Patrick Henry was such a man. At a critical time and in one historic speech he voiced the sentiments of the patriots who touched off the revolution. John Wilkes Booth was also a headliner for a day when he brought the benign leadership of the immortal Lincoln to an untimely end.

It is not necessary for a person to live a long life in the service of the Lord in order to be effective, as we shall see this week. He may fulfil God's purpose for his life in only a brief moment in time. The important thing is to be faithful and alert to the opportunity God gives him. Nor does it follow that a man must have a long record of evildoing to merit God's condemnation. To fail the Lord in a crucial moment, even an otherwise good man, may set the kingdom of God back for many years.

All such men live in the annals of time, but not all of them are assured eternal life.

Sunday
Hobab
Numbers 10:29-32

"Do not leave us, I pray you, for you know how we are to encamp in the wilderness, and you will serve as eyes for us" (v. 31).

When some cynic says, "Money will buy anything," he is only displaying his very limited and prejudiced knowledge of human response. To be sure there are people who respond only to the lures of the highest bidders, but most people will respond to something more than a generous bank account for their services.

Moses learned this simple truth when he was bidding for a guide to lead the people of Israel through the wilderness into the Promised Land. He had picked Hobab, his brother-in-law, for this responsible assignment. Hobab knew all the trails, and most important, he knew the watering places in the desert. A man with Hobab's knowledge and experience was indispensable.

But Hobab was not the adventurous kind. He was at home in the sheep business. He knew the market and was confident of his future. So he said, "I will not go; I will depart to my own land and to my kindred" (v. 30). In other words Hobab said, "I'm going home."

But Moses was not to be denied. He changed his appeal. "We need you," he said. "You know the dangers that lie ahead of these people; you know the trails through these mountains and desert. We need you "as eyes." He concluded his appeal with—"Whatever good the Lord will do to us, the same will we do to you" (v. 32).

This was an appeal for service and faith. "You will serve as eyes for us" speaks of an important and responsible job. There are few appeals as potent as an important and significant job. But there was also an appeal to faith. "Whatever good the Lord will do to us" puts the whole matter of reward and compensation on faith that the Lord will provide.

This appeal Hobab could not resist.

Questions for Meditation: What kind of a job appeals most to you? Adventure? Use of power? Good pay? A chance to serve people? Doing what you please? Short hours?

Prayer: Our Father, we pray that we may ever be responsive to opportunities to serve you. Use our talents, our experience, and our knowledge to serve your kingdom. Teach us that our value to your kingdom is not measured only by our ability, but by our dependence upon you. Amen.

Monday
Jethro
Exodus 18:10-24

> *Now I know that the Lord is greater than all gods, because he delivered the people from under the hand of the Egyptians, when they dealt arrogantly with them (v. 11).*

Jethro played a significant role in Moses' life at several points. First, he gave Moses a home and a job during the time when God was getting him ready for leadership. He changed

Moses from an exile and a fugitive to a settled family man with Jethro's daughter as his wife. He reposed great confidence in him when he encouraged him to follow the Lord's call to lead the people of Israel out of Egyptian bondage.

But most significant was his help in organizing the new nation. He taught Moses that he could not hope to adjudicate all Israel's problems; that only organization and selected and competent leaders could do this. He proposed a heirarchy of judges, all responsible to Moses, that would relieve him of the tedious, strength-consuming tasks of leadership, but retain in Moses' hands the long-range policy decisions which should guide the nation. Jethro's advice stamps him as a very modern administrator. Moses thus became one of the first democratic administrators in history.

Question for Meditation: Moses got his good advice from a nomad in the desert. He might have spurned it as coming from an inexperienced shepherd. How would you decide whether God's leadership is behind the advice you get?

Prayer: Our Father, help us to see that we can serve you best when we join our efforts with others who also seek to do your will. May we stand beside all those who have committed themselves to you. May we be more interested in the results we achieve, than in the credit we receive for our part in the doing. Amen.

Tuesday

Eliezer
Genesis 24:1-21

"O Lord, God of my master Abraham, grant me success today, I pray thee, and show steadfast love to my master Abraham" (v. 12).

Eliezer was a slave to Abraham whom he had acquired in Damascus. Abraham made him the chief over all his business. He entrusted to him his most personal problems.

We are not surprised to hear Eliezer praying to Abraham's God. Although he was reared among pagan gods in a foreign land, his long association with Abraham won him to the worship and obedience of the Lord God Jehovah. Abraham's devotion was not a nominal thing (go to church on Sunday and ignore God the rest of the week). He practiced his devotion to God before all his servants, and he lived consistent with his profession.

Eliezer was very anxious to carry out his master's instructions, and lest he might not select the right maiden, he asks the Lord to do it for him. In his prayer he proposed a sign by which the Lord could tell him which maiden he was to select for the wife of his master's son. When Rebecca responded to his request for a drink by saying, "Drink, and I will water your camels also," he was assured that this was God's selection.

The sign Eliezer proposed not only revealed God's approval of Rebecca, but it showed that she was a most unusual woman —generous, pleasant, and sympathetic not only with Eliezer's needs, but his animals' also. She was eager to be of service and completely unselfish. This was indeed the kind of a wife his master would want for his only son.

It is always appropriate to pray for God's guidance when engaged in an important mission.

Questions for Meditation: Do you think it proper to proposition God? Say to God: "If you will do this for me, I will do that for you." Do you think it proper to make God prove himself—if you are calling me to the mission field, open the door?

Prayer: Our Father, make us conscious of our limitations without you, and make us receptive to your leadership. Our experience and understanding is so fragmentary and yours is so universal, that we would rely on the guidance of your Holy Spirit in any important missions on which you send us. Amen.

Wednesday

Nathan

2 Samuel 12:1-10

Nathan said to David, "You are the man" (v. 7).

Sin is an ugly word. Most of us never use it in reference to our own lives. We use it mostly in the plural form—sins. In this way we avoid talking about our sin specifically.

The Bible never shrugs sin off as being unimportant. It says emphatically that "the wages of sin is death" and "the soul that sinneth shall die." Sin will not go unpunished. Sinners are outside the kingdom. They are alienated from God.

One sin always leads to another. David's first sin was covetousness. He wanted Uriah's wife. This led to the second sin—adultery, and this finally ended in murder.

Nathan was a dedicated servant of the Lord. He might have remonstrated about telling the king that he was a sinner, but without hesitation he obeyed the Lord and confronted David with his sin. It is interesting to note that Nathan led David to condemn himself. It was not necessary for him to elaborate on the seriousness of his sin. David did that himself.

The success of Nathan's mission is revealed when David said, "I have sinned against the Lord" (v. 13). The objective of Christian witnessing is to bring conviction of sin to the sinner. Confession is prerequisite to forgiveness.

Questions for Meditation: When you see a friend committing a grievous sin, should you call it to his attention? Why, or why not?

Prayer: Our Father, help us to be conscious of the repulsiveness of sin in your sight. There is no way you can look on sin with complacency; we must rid ourselves of it, and this can only be done by accepting the sacrifice of the Lord Jesus for the remission of sin. We appeal to your grace and mercy in the forgiveness of our sins. Amen.

Thursday

Caiaphas

Matthew 26:57-68; John 11:47-53

"It is expedient for you that one man should die for the people, and that the whole nation should not perish" (John 11:50).

With the raising of Lazarus from the dead, Jesus gained such stature that even some of the Jewish rulers were attracted to him. Accordingly Caiaphas, the high priest, called the Sanhedrin into counsel. "If we let him go on thus, every one will believe in him," he said. After much discussion, Caiaphas closed the meeting with the verdict that it is "expedient" that Jesus should die.

This was Caiaphas, the responsible leader of the religious and moral community in Jerusalem; Caiaphas, the leader of the highest Jewish authority; Caiaphas, who was ready to, and eventually did, violate every official and ethical principle and tradition of Jewish jurisprudence in order to achieve his predetermined verdict of death. To secure the death sentence he eventually introduced the testimony of false witnesses; he appealed to Jewish prejudices; he distorted the facts; he denied Jesus any semblance of defense; he conducted his pseudocourt at night, contrary to all established legal procedure; he ranted and raved, and tore his priestly robes in pretended shock at what he called Jesus' "blasphemy." And the Sanhedrin did his bidding.

Eventually they brought Jesus to the Roman governor, who alone could pronounce the death sentence, but he was not brought on the charge of blasphemy, but on a charge of "perverting our nation." They did this without introducing the slightest evidence to prove the charge. When Pilate could find no fault in him, they redoubled their frenzy and emotions to shout: "Away with him!" "Crucify, crucify him!"

"And their voices prevailed." Pilate pronounced sentence that their demands should be granted. Caiaphas had played his bitter role and was satisfied—but did he sleep that night?

Questions for Meditation: Was Caiaphas doing the will of God when he prosecuted Jesus to the cross? Does the objective of an action ever determine whether it is right or wrong?

Prayer: Our Father, we pray that we may not crucify our Lord anew by our stubborn and wilful refusal to acknowledge him. There is no place for hatred, violence, and vengeance in our lives. Fill us with the spirit of love and kindness and mercy, and forgive our transgressions. Amen.

Friday
Simon of Cyrene
Mark 15:21; Luke 23:26

They came upon a man of Cyrene, Simon by name; this man they compelled to carry his cross (Matt 27:32).

Simon of Cyrene is introduced to us as a "passer-by." He was doubtless a devout Jew who was making a pilgrimage from his home in Libya in North Africa to participate in the Passover in Jerusalem. Attracted by the tumult, he joined the crowd that was following the crucifixion procession to Calvary outside the city.

Jesus was staggering under the heavy cross that he was expected to carry to the place of the crucifixion. The Roman soldiers impressed Simon into service to carry the cross for Jesus. The record says he was "compelled." This does not mean that Simon had refused to carry it. It means only that he had no choice in the matter. We would like to believe that Simon assumed this burden gladly because of his sympathy for Jesus whose human strength was overtaxed.

There is no record that Simon had had any previous experience with Jesus. Did he witness Jesus' triumphal entry into

Jerusalem the previous Sunday? Did he hear Jesus as he taught in the Temple on Monday and Tuesday? Could he have been in the courtyard while Jesus was on trial Thursday night —perhaps warming himself by the fire with Peter?

Whatever Simon's previous contact with Jesus might have been, he doubtless became one of his followers. Mark tells us that he was the father of Rufus and Alexander. Both of these men were later warmly commended by Paul. Simon had a firsthand experience with Jesus which led to a Christian home and introduced his two boys to Jesus too. Rufus and Alexander became outstanding leaders in the early church—probably in Ephesus and Rome.

Questions for Meditation: What is a father's responsibility for leading his children to the Lord? Do you think he should set an example, or leave it to their mother and their Sunday School teachers?

Prayer: Our Father, impress us into your service that we may accept some of the burden of our Lord and Saviour, as he offers his saving grace to those outside the kingdom. Help us to witness to his sacrifice on the cross for the redemption of sinners. Amen.

Joseph of Arimathea
Mark 15:42-47; John 19:38-42

There was a man named Joseph . . . . He was a member of the council, a good and righteous man, who had not consented to their [the council's] purpose and deed, and he was looking for the kingdom of God. This man went to Pilate and asked for the body of Jesus (Luke 23:50-52).

Joseph was a man of wealth and prestige. Matthew tells us that he was a "rich man." Mark and Luke tell us that he was a member of the Sanhedrin. Mark tells us that he was respected —namely that he had great influence with his associates, although he had not consented to the condemnation of Jesus. He apparently was known to Pilate as a responsible person since he acceded to his request without question. Matthew and John agree that he was a follower of Jesus, but John says it was a secret discipleship because "of fear of the Jews."

Matthew tells us that the tomb was Joseph's own—a new one in which no one had ever lain. It was hewn from solid rock. John tells us that he was joined in the burial preparation by Nicodemus, who had come to see Jesus by night. These two men provided a dignified and honorable burial for Jesus, even if they were both, at best, secret disciples, and neither of them, according to the available records, ever came forward and publicly acknowledged their discipleship.

Joseph rendered an important service to a dead Jesus, but did he ever serve a living Christ? To encourage the followers of Jesus is good, but not good enough. Discipleship demands confession and faith. Secret discipleship falls short of Jesus' demands. "For whoever is ashamed of me and of my words, . . . of him will the Son of man also be ashamed, when he comes in the glory of his Father" (Mark 8:38).

Meet the Nameless Immortals

More than any other book, the Bible tells the stories of nameless people who have left an indelible mark on the history of the world. Who has not heard about the rich young ruler, or the good Samaritan, or the thief on the cross? Many of the events recorded in the Gospels do not disclose the names of those who participated in them. The identity of the person in the incident was less important to the writers of the Gospels than the display of Jesus' power or the deep import of his teachings.

Jesus himself avoided personal acclaim resulting from his miracles. Again and again he cautioned his followers to "tell no one" what he had done. He taught his disciples, "Do not let your left hand know what your right hand is doing" (Matt.

6:3). The highest form of unselfish service is the gift or service that is bestowed anonymously. The giver of such a gift or service is saying that he does not want recognition for the gift, nor any reward for his generosity.

Many community services are rendered because the doing of them is good for the business of the donor. Such services are not to be depreciated, but they do not come within the definition Jesus sets for generosity. There are people who employ press agents to tell the world what good and helpful services they are rendering to the community. About these Jesus said, "Truly, they have their reward" (Matt 6:2). It would be better to be nameless than to sound the trumpet in order to be praised by men.

Sunday
The Lad with the Loaves and Fishes
John 6:5-14

"There is a lad here who has five barley loaves and two fish; but what are they among so many?" (v. 9).

According to Shakespeare "some [men] are born great, some achieve greatness, and some have greatness thrust upon them." Certainly the lad with the bread and fish had no idea of seeking fame when he left his home in the morning with five little loaves to go fishing. He had done this many mornings during his few years. This day the fish were not biting. Having fished most of the day, he had caught only two small ones. Hunger was beckoning him to prepare his fish and eat his loaves, when he saw a multitude of people along the shore. Boyish curiosity impelled him to investigate.

He arrived just as Jesus had sent out a committee to investigate the food resources in order that he might feed the assembled people—five thousand of them. Only the lad had had the foresight to bring his lunch, and he was so astonished by the prospect of feeding the thousands with the contents of his lunch box that he readily contributed what he had. The record tells the story of the feeding, with twelve baskets of food left over. Fame was really thurst upon the lad.

But it was not entirely circumstance that made him famous. It was his readiness to share what little he had with those in need that enabled Jesus to bless his contribution and feed the hungry people. How much we have to share is really not important. If we commit it into the hands of the Lord, it can bless the multitude. When we are tempted to excuse ourselves because we have so little to give, it is important to remember that a little in the hands of the Lord is more than enough to serve those in need.

Questions for Meditation: What small abilities do you have that you think God cannot use? Have you offered them?

Prayer: Our Father, our talents and resources are so few that we are wont to disparage them, and thereby excuse ourselves from serving you. Teach us that what little we can give is enough for you to do the incredible. The obstacle to great things is our reluctance to give, not your power to multiply our gifts. Amen.

Monday
The Widow with Her Mite
Mark 12:41-44

> *They all contributed out of their abundance; but she out of her poverty has put in everything she had, her whole living (v. 44).*

By Jesus' standards the test of a person's generosity is not how much he has given, but how much he has left after the gift. That is to say, Jesus does not expect large gifts from those with modest means, nor is he satisfied with small gifts from those with large means. "To whom much is given," he said, "of him will much be required" (Luke 12:48). Moreover, the value of the gift is measured in the sight of God by the sacrifice it entails for the giver.

Even the large gifts that were cast into the treasury did not store up the treasures in heaven for the givers that the widow's mite stored up for her, because she had given everything she had.

From this story of the widow's mite we gain a clear insight into Jesus' attitude toward giving. It is the spirit in which it is given that counts with the Lord. Paul quotes Jesus as saying, "God loves a cheerful giver." He elaborates this thought by pointing out that "he who sows sparingly will also reap sparingly, and he who sows bountifully will also reap bountifully" (2 Cor. 9:6-7).

It is safe to say that the widow did not expect the heavens to open and shower her with prosperity because of her sacrificial gift. To give in expectation of material return is to spoil the spirit of the gift. When Jesus said, "The measure you give will be the measure you get back" (Luke 6:38), he did not necessarily refer to material measure. God has many blessings with which he can bless our generosity. In God's sight, many of these available blessings are far more important than material blessings. The true giver gives with a faith that the Lord will give him the blessing that he needs most.

Questions for Meditation: Did you ever make a gift to the Lord that represented a real sacrifice? What did it cost you? Be honest.

Prayer: Our Father, we pray that the gifts we bring to you may be the true measure of our gratitude for the blessings with which you have blessed us. Forbid that we should withhold from you the firstfruits of our earnings because we want to be more comfortable. Amen.

Tuesday
The Man Born Blind
John 9:1-34

"One thing I know, that though I was blind, now I see"
(v. 25).

It is hard to successfully refute a personal testimony about what God has done for one. No wonder the Pharisees were stopped cold when the once blind man insisted, "Though I was blind, now I see." One cannot argue with facts plainly evident.

The Pharisees did their best to trap this man in theological jargon. He [Jesus] cannot be from God because he does not keep the sabbath. What do you say about that? We know he is a sinner, so how can he be from God? They tried to cast doubt about his own identity, but he cut that short by saying, "I am he." At no time did he permit himself to be drawn into controversy. He stuck to his personal testimony—"Though I was blind, now I see."

When Billy Graham was asked about the "God is dead" hysteria, he is reported to have said, "Impossible, I talked to him only this morning." Christian witnesses do well to confine their testimony to their own experience. Peter put it this way: "We cannot but speak of what we have seen and heard" (Acts 4:20). Jesus himself said: "We speak of what we know, and bear witness to what we have seen" (John 3:11). No testimony is as convincing as a personal experience. "One thing I know, that though I was blind [spiritually], now I see."

Questions for Meditation: Has your experience with the Lord been so real that nothing can shake it? When did you last tell anyone about it?

Prayer: Our Father, save us from argument and dispute. Let the words of our mouth be acceptable to you. Help us to proclaim your grace and mercy toward all who believe and call upon you for forgiveness. Amen.

The Little Slave Girl
2 Kings 5:2-5

"Would that my lord were with the prophet who is in Samaria! He would cure him of his leprosy" (v. 3).

One does not have to be a high imperial potentate to be the source of good advice. Nor is it necessary to be a courier of the king's palace to be the bearer of good news.

Naaman was the supreme commander of the most powerful army of his day, but he was a leper. The little Hebrew girl was a slave in Naaman's home. These two had nothing in common, but the little girl had something that Naaman desperately needed—human compassion and a faith in her God.

Her compassion prompted her to speak to her mistress with advice about curing Naaman's leprosy. Her faith in God led her to recommend the prophet of God who resided in the land from which she had been evicted. Human need and the power of God met in the heart of the little girl. She and she alone held the key to Naaman's need, and she was not negligent in sharing what she had.

All about us people, both great and small, are afflicted with something more deadly than leprosy—sin. Every Christian knows that there is only one remedy for this affliction—faith in the Lord Jesus Christ, and there is only one place to go to be cleansed from this affliction—the cross of Jesus. Everyone who has experienced God's grace and forgiveness holds the key to the needs of a sin-cursed world. We need compassion for lost sinners, and a compulsion to lead them to the only one who can forgive their sins and heal their souls.

As a result of the slave girl's witness, Naaman was not only cured physically, but he became a follower of the Lord God Jehovah, and was cured spiritually.

Questions for Meditation: Is there someone who will not be healed of his spiritual leprosy unless you direct him to the Great Physician? Do you have as much compassion for lost sinners as the slave girl had for a sick man?

Prayer: Our Father, where else can we advise people who are in need of sin-cleansing to go? You have the words of eternal life. Give us the compassion for sin-sick people that will impel us to direct them to the Saviour of the world. Amen.

Thursday
The Samaritan Woman
John 4:7-27

Many Samaritans from that city believed in him because of the woman's testimony (v. 39).

When Jesus said: "The sabbath was made for man, not man for the sabbath" (Mark 2:27), he stated a fundamental principle of his life and teaching: nothing is more important than people, especially people in need—not even the divinely established institution of the sabbath.

No wonder he did not hesitate to break some of the age-old customs of his day when he was found talking with a woman in public—and an outcast at that—and most incredible of all, a Samaritan. One count against the woman was enough, but two, that was inexcusable. Even the woman recognized the breach as far as her nationality was concerned, "How is it that you, a Jew, ask a drink of me, a woman of Samaria?"

It is noteworthy that she carefully abstained from surprise that he would talk to a woman with her unsavory reputation. But Jesus, recognizing her great moral and spiritual need, faced her with her marital history, together with her present abandonment of all moral restraints.

People are always eager to change the subject when they are confronted with their moral lapses, so this woman quickly turned the conversation to safer topics—one the Jews and Samaritans had kicked around for centuries. Where is the proper place to worship God? On Samaria's Mount Gerizim or in Jerusalem?

In reply to her question, Jesus expressed one of the most penetrating insights into the nature of God to be found in all literature. The place is not important, Jesus explained. *How* God is worshiped is very important, for, said he, "God is spirit, and those who worship him must worship in spirit and truth" (v. 24).

Once more she sought to evade the personal implications of what Jesus was saying to her. "I know," she ventured, "that Messiah is coming (he who is called Christ); . . . he will show us all things" (v. 25). She was not really interested in the coming of the Messiah, but this was such a far-off event it seemed safe to talk about it. But Jesus, refusing to be diverted, astonished her with a quiet announcement: "I who speak to you am he" (v. 26). In effect Jesus was asking, "What are you going to do now?"

She was not long in answering. Confused and shaken, she hurriedly returned to her village and broadcast her experience. "Can this be the Christ?" she challenged.

Questions for Meditation: Are you worshiping God in truth—really letting him have his way in your life? What are you holding back?

Prayer: Our Father, often we are so conscious of our moral and spiritual lapses that we are ashamed to face your holiness. Cleanse us from our unrighteousness and the sin that besets us so easily. Help us to face you with a contrite and humble heart, so that you can restore us to your fellowship. Amen.

Friday
The Thief on the Cross
Luke 23:39-43

"We are receiving the due reward of our deeds; but this man has done nothing wrong." And he said, "Jesus, remember me when you come in your kingly power" (vv. 41-42).

The voice of the thief on the cross was the only voice raised in behalf of Jesus on Calvary. How tragic that the only voice of compassion for the Saviour came from a criminal!

But this was no ordinary criminal. He showed remarkable insight into the character and mission of Jesus. First, he forgot his own present suffering to think about his destiny, which was only minutes away. Second, he did not ask to be saved from his cross, like his partner. He accepted the justice of the cross for him, but he saw something more in Jesus, and asked to be reconciled with him in his kingdom. Third, he had a surprising faith. We have the record and testimony of two thousand years of Christian witnessing to support our faith, but the thief had only this brief encounter with Jesus on the cross beside him. There was no "if" in his plea to Jesus. He said: *"When* you come into your kingdom." He had faith in Jesus as a person. He had faith in his power. He relied on his promise. Can you match such faith?

The two thieves on the crosses that day represent the entire human race: some rail, refusing the Saviour; some accept forgiveness; some seek only physical well-being; some seek spiritual well-being; some think only of the present; some look to the hereafter; some question Christ—"If you can"; some believe—"When you come."

Question for Meditation: This thief knew nothing of creeds, doctrine, or theology. He knew only his faith in Jesus. Paul said: "Believe on the Lord Jesus Christ." Why do we make salvation seem so complicated?

Prayer: Our Father, we are so grateful that it is never too late to acknowledge the Saviour; but Lord, forbid that we should waste all the years of our lives when we might have been serving you, only to come at the eleventh hour to claim your redemption and mercy. Amen.

Saturday
The Father of the Epileptic Boy
Mark 9:14-29

"If you can do anything, have pity on us and help us" (*v. 22*).

Human extremity is frequently God's opportunity. Many a man has been won to faith in God because there was nowhere else to go. A house-afire religion is at best a reluctant admission of human inability to cope with life.

The father of this boy had exhausted all the possibilities of curing him. He even brought him to the disciples and "they were not able." He had been rebuffed so many times that even his approach to Jesus for help reflected the uncertainty in his mind. Perhaps this was just another false hope. "If you can do anything," was his qualifying petition.

Jesus had to establish first of all a firm basis of faith. "All things are possible to him who believes," he assured the father. Faith is a prerequisite for God's answer to petitions. How many times are our petitions blocked by a mental "if you can do anything"? Jesus promised, "Whatever you ask in prayer, you will receive, if you have faith" (Matt. 21:22). Unbelief is the cemetery of many petitions.

Meet the
Might-have-beens

The highways of history are strewn with the wreckage of men and women who "might have been" towering giants in the service of the Lord. Some of these, like Judas Iscariot, attached themselves to wrong causes. Some of them, like Samson, played with evil until they were unable to extricate themselves. Others, like Methuselah, just frittered away their time and opportunity, doing nothing of significance. Still others, like Nicodemus, knew what they should do, and fully intended to do it sometime, but indecision defeated them.

What a different world this might have been if Alexander, or Caesar, or Napoleon had enlisted in God's army and fought for the kingdom of God, rather than their own power and glory. It is said that Alexander wept because there were no more worlds to conquer. It is too bad that he did not recognize the world of evil as a fit antagonist for his very considerable talents for fighting.

This author would not want to prejudge these might-have-beens, but based on the evidence at hand they did not measure up to their opportunities for service which God gave them. Nor would we depreciate the good which some of them did; but they failed, according to the record, to accomplish what God expected of them. The test of a man is not how he stands in his own estimation, nor in the esteem of his fellowmen, but how he stands in the sight of God. "Man looks on the outward appearance, but the Lord looks on the heart" (1 Sam. 16:7). Jesus cried over Jerusalem, "How often would I have gathered your children together . . . and you would not!" (Matt. 23:37). Here was a whole city of might-have-beens.

Sunday

Nicodemus
John 3:1-21

"If I have told you earthly things and you do not believe, how can you believe if I tell you heavenly things?" (v. 12).

Nicodemus was an intellectual who would accept nothing that did not agree with what he knew about the natural world. If he were living today he would insist on putting everything in a test tube to determine whether it is true or false. Jesus recognized this limitation and told him in effect, "You have been born into the natural world, and you see and understand the natural world, but you must be reborn into the spiritual world if you would understand spiritual things."

There is nothing to indicate that Nicodemus was ever "born anew." He came to Jesus as an inquirer looking for something —he knew not what. He thought his intellectual processes should open the spiritual world, but they did not help. He had yet to learn what Jesus had told the Samaritan woman at Jacob's well, that "God is [a] spirit, and those who worship him must worship [him] in spirit and truth" (4:24).

It seems that Nicodemus was still searching on the day of Jesus' crucifixion, when he came forward to assist in his burial. Nicodemus felt that somehow Jesus held the key to his yearning for something better, but he would not trust the Lord and commit himself to what Paul called "the foolishness of God"— for "the foolishness of God is wiser than men" (1 Cor. 1:25).

Nicodemus might have been another Paul. He was highly educated, held a high position, was respected, and was seriously concerned about the kingdom of God, but he would not become an all-out disciple. It is not enough to give intellectual assent to the teachings of Jesus. It is not enough to join the church, read the Bible, pray, or be baptized. Jesus requires more than complimentary phrases—"Rabbi, we know that you are a teacher come from God." How much better, if he could have said, "My Lord, and my God."

Questions for Meditation: Is education and intellectual ability an asset or a liability in serving the Lord? If his intellectualism was so important to Nicodemus, why did it not fill his craving for something better?

Prayer: Our Father, we pray that our intelligence may give us a truer insight into things spiritual and not be an obstacle to faith in you. Combine our minds and hearts in our quest for your truth, and let your Spirit dwell in us to rule over our lives. Amen.

Monday
Methuselah
Genesis 5:21-27

"Thus all the days of Methuselah were nine hundred and sixty-nine years; and he died" (v. 27).

Methuselah had a wonderful father. The record says he "walked with God." We can assume from this that Enoch's son had the advantages of a God-fearing home; that his father's search for God's will was real and constant; that he did those things that were pleasing to God, both in his vocation and in his home. None of these virtues are recorded about the son. The record simply states that Methusaleh lived more years than any other person in history, that he "had sons and daughters" and that "he died." Can it be possible that a man can live more than nine hundred years and in all that time do nothing which would merit the approval of God and be worth recording in his biography. What wasted years!

How did Methuselah spend those years? Did he fritter away his time and talents whittling at the corner store? Was he engaged in a business that God could not honor? Was he occupied with many little diversions, none of them evil, that were neither useful nor constructive?

His grandson was Noah, who also "walked with God," and built the ark according to God's instructions. Methuselah lived throughout the period when the ark was under construction, and died only two years before the flood. Did he help build the ark? Or was he among the scoffers who ridiculed Noah? The record tells us that God decided to have Noah build the ark because "the earth was corrupt." Did this include Methuselah?

What a difference he could have made upon the people of his time, if he had devoted his long life wholeheartedly to the service of God. Unfortunately the record on this is silent.

Tuesday

Samson

Judges 16:18-31

He did not know that the Lord had left him (v. 20).

Samson, like so many people today, lived so much with evil that he lost his ability to distinguish between right and wrong. He had every opportunity to be an inspiring leader for God. Instead he became a showman, dominated by lust and violence.

Samson was brought up in a devout home, dedicated by his mother from birth to the service of God. The record says "the Lord blessed him" (13:24). But Samson never committed himself to service for God. Not once did he call on Israel to repent and mend her ways; to return to Jehovah; to forsake their pagan worship. Only after he was blinded, humiliated, and weary of life did he recognize that the Lord had given him his phenomenal strength, and he asked God that it be restored to him just once more.

Delilah, his pagan wife, was the temptress that caused his downfall. He was so sure that he could command any situation that he flirted with temptation. Gradually she wore down his resistance so that his "soul was vexed to death." What tears and sweet-talk could not do, nagging accomplished. He told her the secret of his unusual strength. Shorn of his long locks, he was helpless before his tormentors, and, pathetically, "he did not know that the Lord had left him."

Like Samson, we flirt with evil so long that we are unaware that our power with God is gone. Prayers go unanswered; peace of mind and heart vanish; the joy of living in Christ is no more. Little by little we find ourselves weary and blinded, grinding corn at the Philistine mill like Samson, who might have been an inspiring flame for God.

Lot
Genesis 13:3-13; 19:1-29

"But he lingered; so the men seized him and his wife and his two daughters by the hand, the Lord being merciful to him, and they brought him forth and set him outside the city" (Gen. 19:16).

Lot came from a long line of worshipers of the Lord God Jehovah. He was a protégé of his uncle Abraham, and should have been influenced by the faith of this remarkable patriarch. But there is no record that Lot ever acknowledged a personal relationship to the Lord. Not once did he call on the Lord in prayer.

When Abraham suggested that they separate their herds, and offered Lot his choice of grazing land, "Lot lifted up his eyes, and saw that the Jordan valley was well watered everywhere like the garden of the Lord." So he chose the Jordan valley and "moved his tent as far as Sodom."

It is significant that he chose this most wicked of all cities as his headquarters. He soon became embroiled in the tribal rivalries of the area, and was taken prisoner, both he and his entire household. Abraham had to organize a posse of three hundred men to pursue the abductors and rescue him.

Even when the Lord's angels came to save Lot from the doomed city of Sodom, he was so attached to his wicked environment that he had to be led out of the city forcibly. There are few more tragic situations than when a member of a devout, God-fearing family is cold and unresponsive to God's love and care. Lot had all the possibilities of his Uncle Abraham, but he lacked faith in the Lord, and in the end this is all he really needed to become an inspiring voice for God.

Question for Meditation: Is it true that the kind of associates we seek reveals the kind of people we are?

Thursday
Saul
1 Samuel 15:1-23, 35

"Because you have rejected the word of the Lord, he has also rejected you from being king" (v. 23).

Saul was a tall, handsome young man who looked the part of a king. When the people first saw him, they shouted spontaneously, "Long live the king!" But Saul had never committed himself to serve the Lord. He always referred to the Lord as Samuel's God. His power and position soon went to his head, and he became arrogant and did not seek the will of the Lord.

When Samuel came as a messenger of the Lord to advise him in his war against the Amalekites, he deliberately disobeyed the Lord. He spared the king of the Amalekites to gloat over him, and, contrary to God's specific instruction, he saved the best of all the Amalekite possessions as spoils of war. In addition to his disobedience, he was filled with vengeance and covetousness. He became so jealous of David's popularity with the people after he had slain Goliath, that he sought to kill him.

Saul was sponsored by the aged Samuel who had guided Israel for forty years. He had the personality and the leadership the position required, but he was not committed to the Lord. His vanity, stubbornness, arrogance, and selfishness destroyed him. He might have been a great king. He proved himself a weakling. In the end he took his own life. Except the Lord controls a man's life, he can never be all that God meant for him to be.

Question for Meditation: Can a man be faithful to the Lord if he has not committed himself personally to serve him?

Judas Iscariot
Matthew 27:3-10

"I have sinned in betraying innocent blood.".. . . *And throwing down the pieces of silver in the temple, he departed; and he went and hanged himself (vv. 4-5).*

The failure of Judas to commit himself irrevocably to Jesus' discipleship must have been an outstanding disappointment to Jesus. He saw in Judas great potential leadership. He recognized in him a genius for organization and administration. Judas established himself as something of a business manager of the little group of Jesus' followers. He kept them in provisions. He was alert to the material needs of people. He managed the meager funds that were offered by sympathetic people, and made them suffice for Jesus' needs.

But Judas could never get the idea of a spiritual kingdom. In fact, his fellow disciples were slow to accept this interpretation of Jesus' mission until after the resurrection. If Jesus was the promised Messiah, Judas reasoned, it must be that he would restore the power and glory of David's kingdom. To this he committed himself completely.

Why did Judas betray the Master? Bible scholars have never agreed. Could it be that he thought by jeopardizing Jesus' life, he could force Jesus to proclaim an insurrection against Rome and restore the Jewish nation? If so it was a tragic miscalculation.

History records Judas among its most tragic failures. Here was a man who spent three years with Jesus, and yet missed his opportunity to share the building of the kingdom of God to which Jesus had called him. Knowing about Jesus, listening to his words, and watching his activities is not enough. Judas had never committed himself, without reservation, to following Jesus. Because of this he never had a part in proclaiming God's plan for redeeming lost sinners.

Questions for Meditation: How many people participate in all the activities of the Christian church, but never really commit themselves to the Lord Jesus? What more is required?

Prayer: Our Father, sometimes we are so obsessed with doing what we want to do, we fail to hear your voice as you try to guide our footsteps. Grant that we may ask daily, "Lord, what do you want me to do?"

Saturday
The Rich Young Ruler
Mark 10:17-22

> *"If you would be perfect, go, sell what you possess and give to the poor, and you will have treasure in heaven; and come, follow me." When the young man heard this he went away sorrowful; for he had great possessions (Matt. 19:21-22).*

Jesus confronted this young man with a destiny-determining decision: "Which means most to you, eternal life or a fat bank account?"

There is no evidence that Jesus ever frowned upon wealth as such. He was always concerned about how it was obtained and how it was used. In this instance he was concerned about the young man's attachment to his wealth, and the test Jesus proposed was to test his heart's real desire. Unfortunately, he flunked the test.

He must have had a winning personality—a clean life record—qualifications for great service. Jesus wanted him among his followers. He saw in him great possibilities. He might have been another Paul or a Barnabas or a Timothy. He might have written another gospel, or written letters to young churches. The Lord sent Paul west into Europe. He might have sent this young man east into India or China. How greatly was the future of the kingdom of God retarded because this young man chose to go his selfish way. Jesus voiced his disappointment when he commented wistfully, "How hard it will be for those who have riches to enter the kingdom of God!" All Jesus asked the young man to do was to put his wealth in the correct perspective to other values in life. God will not compete with material posessions for first place in a man's heart.

Questions for Meditation: Jesus put his finger on the young man's weakness—money. What is your weakness? Are you willing to give the Lord first place?

Prayer: Our Father, we live in a materialistic society, and it is so easy to be swayed by the allurement of material things. Help us, O Lord, to recognize the priority of spiritual things, and keep these two worlds in correct perspective. Amen.

Meet the Outcasts

It is a terrible experience for one to be an outcast. It may be only a temporary quarantine to protect the health of the public; it may be assignment to an asylum for the well-being of the patient; it may be imprisonment for being a public menace; it may be ostracism for being morally or socially unacceptable. Whatever the circumstances that compel the separation of man from his fellowman, it is nothing compared with his separation from God. To be an outcast from God is the supreme tragedy that can befall a human being.

To be an outcast does not necessarily mean eternal separation from God. Sin separates from God, but Jesus said: "I came not to call the righteous, but sinners" (Mark 2:17). It is not God's will that anyone should be cast out. The Bible says:

"The Lord . . . is forbearing toward you, not wishing that any should perish, but that all should reach repentance" (2 Peter 3:9).

The compassionate heart of Jesus went out to all outcasts. He cleansed the leper; he restored the mentally unbalanced; he forgave the morally ostracized; he set at liberty those who were bound by their passions or prejudice. His invitation was to all "who labor and are heavy-laden"; his promise, "I will give you rest" (Matt. 11:28).

Sunday

Nebuchadnezzar

Daniel 4:28-37

"The kingdom has departed from you, and you shall be driven from among men, and your dwelling shall be with the beasts of the field . . . until you have learned that the Most High rules the kingdom of men" (v. 31-32).

"Pride goes before destruction, and a haughty spirit before a fall" (Prov. 16:18). An unseemly pride led to Nebuchadnezzar's fall. "My mighty power" and "the glory of my majesty" expresses the vanity of this monarch, whose consuming passion was to build vast monuments to his own greatness. Daniel had warned him of his impending fall—"Break off your sins by practicing righteousness, and your iniquities by showing mercy to the oppressed" (v. 27).

Nebuchadnezzar was granted one year to show repentance for his vanity and pride. He did not respond. Unseemly pride and vanity can only be described as madness. Not until this king humbled himself before the Lord did his sanity return to him.

When we think of the greatness of America, what is our standard of values? Are we impressed with our deep spiritual lives? Do we talk about our faith in God's leadership? Can we take pride in our moral standards? Are we a people whose dominating desire it is to bring in the kingdom of God?

Or do we glory in our power—economic and military? How impressed are we with size—gross national product? Do we gauge our greatness by our bank deposits, wage scales, stock markets, government operations, natural resources, automobiles, television sets, and the like?

Nebuchadnezzar would have included all these under—"my mighty power" and "the glory of my majesty." When will we regain our reason and acknowledge that "the Most High rules the kingdom of men and gives it to whom he will" (v. 32)?

"You shall remember the Lord your God, for it is he who gives you power to get wealth. . . . And if you forget the Lord your God and go after other gods and serve them and worship them, . . . you shall surely perish" (Deut. 8:18-19).

Questions for Meditation: What counts most with you? Your bank balance? Your investments? Your job? Your social position? Your family? Your church? Your education? Your friends? Your Saviour?

Prayer: Our Father, we humbly acknowledge our dependence on you for all the blessings we enjoy. May we never be so thoughtless as to conclude that our blessings are the rewards for our ability, our goodness, or our superior workmanship. Amen.

Monday
Ishmael
Genesis 21:8-21

> *"Cast out this slave woman with her son; for the son of this slave woman shall not be heir with my son Isaac" (v. 10).*

Sarah became impatient and concluded that when the Lord promised them a son in their old age, he had taken on more than he could do. So she devised a plan whereby Abraham should have a son by Hagar, Sarah's handmaiden. This plan proved effective but it was not God's plan.

In due time Sarah bore her own son, Isaac, according to God's promise. But Ishmael, Hagar's son, was the elder, and according to the tradition and custom of that day he was destined to be the heir, not only of Abraham's material possessions, but of his spiritual blessing as well. Sarah was alarmed. She feared the great nation which God had promised Abraham and his descendants would spring from the descendants of Ishmael rather than her son Isaac.

To remedy this situation she devised another plan. Ishmael must be banished from the household of Abraham. He must be cast out, exiled, disinherited. And so Hagar and her son Ishmael "departed, and wandered in the wilderness of Beersheba" (v. 14). But God "was with the lad, and he grew up; he lived in the wilderness" (v. 20).

One wrong frequently calls for another. We tell an untruth and must tell another to explain the first. Sarah's first sin was to question God's ability to fulfil his promise. Then she undertook to do what she thought God could not do. Finally, she had to undo the mischief she had contrived by making the lad Ishmael an outcast.

Note, God not only delivered on his promise, but he "was with the lad, Ishmael." God in his great mercy is not only ready to forgive our transgressions, but he is frequently impelled to ease the consequences of our sin upon the innocent.

Question for Meditation: Ishmael's descendants are the Arabs of today. Do you think their hostility toward Israel is God's punishment for Ishmael's banishment?

Prayer: Our Father, forbid that we should ever question your promises or presume upon your ability to perform them. Your promise to bless us far beyond our capacity to them, if we will pay our obligations to you and obey your commandments, is precious to us beyond our ability to thank you adequately or to serve you. Amen.

Tuesday
Zaccheus
Luke 19:1-10

"He has gone in to be the guest of a man who is a sinner" (v. 7).

Did you ever hear someone say, "You can't change human nature"? Zaccheus was a living refutation of this falsehood. When Jesus enters a person's life he is "a new creation," according to Paul. "The old has passed away, behold, the new has come" (2 Cor. 5:17).

Zaccheus was an outcast in his own community because of his servitude to Rome and his unscrupulous greed in amassing his own fortune. The steps leading to his re-creation are available to everyone: (1) He had a sense of need for something better in life than his possessions could give him. (2) He felt that Jesus could do something about it. (3) He had such a sense of urgency about seeing Jesus that he let nothing stand in his way. (4) He welcomed Jesus' offer to come into his life. (5) He insisted that his wealth should not come between him and the life Jesus offered him. (6) He dedicated his possessions to the service of God and his fellowman—half of his possessions were to be given to the poor, and with the rest he made such restitution as he could to those whom he had wronged in the acquisition of his wealth. (7) He made Jesus "Lord" of his life (cf. v. 8).

To make Jesus Lord of one's life requires positive action—change of objectives; acceptance of Jesus' values in life; obedience; acknowledgment of his lordship before the world; commitment of one's life and possessions; make restitution, where possible, for wrong done to others. To say, "I am sorry," is not enough. One must correct the mischief as far as possible.

Zacchaeus made a choice that day. It determined his whole life thereafter. There is no record that he quit his tax-collecting job. He learned how to be an honest tax collector and a Christian, too. Every Christian should be able to reconcile his vocation with his commitment to Christ.

Question for Meditation: Would you say that no man should have a job that Jesus would not honor and bless?

Prayer: Our Father, we would make every facet of our lives consistent with our commitment to follow you—business, social life, family, recreation. We pray that the image of our discipleship may not be marred by the way we live before our fellowmen. May our conduct be an even better witness than our words. Amen.

Wednesday
The Adultress About to Be Stoned
John 8:1-11

"Let him who is without sin among you be the first to throw a stone at her" (v. 7).

There is a requirement in our judicial system that anyone coming into court to seek redress for grievances, must come with clean hands. The court cannot mete out justice for one when both litigants are guilty.

It takes two to commit adultery. Perhaps Jesus suspected that some of the woman's "customers" were among her self-appointed judges, or perhaps their moral reputation was so shady that they felt they had to put on this exhibition of virtue to sustain their ego. Whatever the circumstances, their concern for the moral climate of the community was not genuine, nor were they concerned about the welfare of the woman.

Moreover, they were willing to use the plight of the unfortunate woman to set a snare whereby they might trap Jesus.

Sin is never so real as when it becomes personal. We can discuss sin in general with glib tongue. Few there are who would defend sin in someone else. But when someone points an accusing finger and says, "Thou art the man," sin becomes personal and we become defensive.

No one was as surprised as the woman's accusers when Jesus dared anyone without sin to cast the first stone. What a parade of sin must have passed through the minds of the accusers! No wonder they slunk out of the picture like whipped dogs until no one was left except Jesus and the woman. Jesus closed the case with an admonition: "Go, and do not sin again."

Question for Meditation: Under what circumstances would you recommend that the formula Jesus used in this instance be applied today?

Prayer: Our Father, help us to examine the sin in our own lives before we point fingers at our erring brothers. There is so much evil in most of us that none of us can condemn the rest of us. Lord, be merciful to me, a sinner. Amen.

Thursday
The Demon-Possessed Exile
Mark 5:2-17

> There met him . . . *a man with an unclean spirit, who lived among the tombs; and no one could bind him . . . even with a chain (v. 2).*

In Mark's day only an evil (unclean) spirit could adequately explain an unbalanced mind. This is not a far-fetched explanation. How better can a personality overbalanced by an overpowering greed or hatred or prejudice be explained than by an "evil spirit"?

Do you know a person who is all kindness and courtesy in public but insufferable at home? Some people are tolerant and generous in their social contacts, but hard and uncompromising in their business relations.

The significance of this episode lies in the fact that such people are not comfortable in the presence of Jesus—"Do not torment me." Whenever a life torn by evil spirits encounters Jesus, he restores balance, sanity, and calmness—"sitting there, clothed and in his right mind."

Note the inevitable distrust of everything possessed by such evil, unholy, and unsocial spirits. How else can it end? The owners of the swine suffered great loss, but note the reactions. First, they did not rejoice over the restored sanity of the demented man. Second, they asked Jesus to leave their community.

What is the well-being of a human being compared with a material loss? Was the price for saving this man too great? Too often when Christ and business come into conflict, Christ is invited out of the situation. But the demon-freed man wanted to stay with Jesus always.

Questions for Meditation: Name some business that would banish Jesus because he would be an obstacle to that business. Does Jesus bless or condemn your business?

Prayer: Our Father, help us to evaluate our lives by Jesus' emphasis on the sacredness of human personality. Nothing takes precedence over that. Come into our lives and restore sanity and a sense of responsibility for those who are torn and frustrated by evil forces. Amen.

Friday

The Man with One Talent

Matthew 25:14-30

"You wicked and slothful servant! . . . you ought to have invested my money with the bankers. . . . So take the talent from him. . . . And cast the worthless servant into the outer darkness" (vv. 26-30).

Obviously everyone is not endowed with the same number of talents. But God does not hold us accountable for talents we do not possess. Note that the one-talent man was not condemned because he had not earned five talents, or even two. He was not cast out because he had squandered his one talent, or made a poor investment, or spent it on himself, or lost it. He was charged with doing nothing. His master called him a "slothful" servant—one who is lazy. The dictionary says "one who is disinclined to work." He was useless.

It is not enough to hoard one's talents. Talents are meant to be used, developed, enlarged by experience and effort. Most of us are one-talent people. We are inclined to say, "there is not much I can do." We are ready to let the many-talented people do the work. Jesus' condemnation is for all such—"You wicked and slothful servants!"

Note, the penalty for uselessness is to be cast out—alienated from God, and the loss of the talent you have. You do not have to be dishonest, profane, violent, or immoral to be cast out—just do nothing, ignore all responsibility to God and man.

Note also the rewards for faithfulness. They are based on maximum effort, not on results. The five- and two-talent men received the same commendation and promise. Each had performed to the extent of his talents. God does not say, "Do as well as John." He says, "Do the best you can with the talent with which you have been endowed."

Saturday

The Useless

Matthew 25:31-46

"As you did it not to one of the least of these, you did it not to me." And they will go away into eternal punishment (vv. 45-46).

Godlessness can only lead to eternal separation from God. "Do not be deceived; God is not mocked, for whatever a man sows, that he will also reap" (Gal. 6:7). But God's condemnation is not limited to overt acts of unrighteousness. The charges against the folks who were cast out and assigned to eternal separation from God consisted exclusively of neglected opportunities to serve the Lord. They were condemned for what they did *not* do. It is possible to be cast out for the sin of doing nothing.

God has a purpose and life plan for everyone, which he will reveal to those who diligently seek to find his will. Sometimes men attempt to evade his will, like Jonah, and God is compelled to use diagreeable measures to keep them from making a tragic mistake. More often men fail to do God's will because they are preoccupied with their own plans, and so they have no time to serve the Lord. Those who were condemned for being useless seem to have been "good people." There is no indication of moral degeneracy. They did not blaspheme the Lord. They did not rebel against him, but they ignored him. It is possible to reject God's mercy and forgiveness by procrastination and delay.

"Today, when you hear his voice, do not harden your hearts as in the rebellion" (Heb. 3:7-8). "Now is the accepted time; behold, now is the day of salvation" (2 Cor. 6:2, KJV).

Question for Meditation: The Bible says that if you do not warn the wicked and they die in their sin, you will be held accountable. How accountable are you?

Meet the Women

Simple gratitude is a rare commodity in the world today. The current insistence on "rights" is incompatible with it. The clamor for privileges and benefits is out of step with it. The philosophy of violence and power is abhorrent to it. Gratitude is a state of the heart. Such a heart asks nothing, but it glories in the blessings others have made possible. Gratitude expressed in a dedicated life is the least anyone can offer the Saviour of the world for his sacrifice on the cross.

Someone has said that every woman should be a disciple of the Lord, if only to express her gratitude for what he has done to raise womanhood to the exalted station it occupies today. Nowhere in the life and teachings of Jesus is there the slightest hint that he looked upon women as second-class persons.

Nowhere does he infer that they are inferior to their husbands. Nowhere does he deny them places of respect and honor. On the contrary his last thought on the cross was to provide for the care of his mother. His first appearance after his resurrection was to Mary Magdalene. He reserved some of his most revealing teaching about God for a public woman at Jacob's well. He rebuked a scribe for criticizing a woman who was showing her gratitude for Jesus' forgiveness of her sins. "Whosoever will may come" included women.

The world has been slow to accept Jesus' standard for womanhood. It took centuries to liberate her from her agelong status of subservience. Even in America it has been less than fifty years since woman's equality was recognized by giving her the privilege of voting. In many states they are still restricted in the disposition of their property without their husband's consent. A double standard of morality for men and women is still countenanced.

Women have not made their transition to a nobler station in life any easier by insisting on copying the vices of men—drinking, smoking, swearing, and the like. In so doing they are accepting a status beneath that which Jesus had in mind for them. The women in this volume were outstanding examples of the best in womanhood in their day, and in ours as well.

Sunday

Miriam

Exodus 15:20-21; Numbers 12:1-10

Then Miriam, . . . the sister of Aaron, took a timbrel in her hand; and all the women went out after her with timbrels and dancing. And Miriam sang to them: "Sing to the Lord, for he has triumphed gloriously; the horse and his rider he has thrown into the sea" (Ex. 15:20-21).

Miriam was off to a good start. She saved the life of her brother Moses, and assured him as a child of the love and

guidance of a mother. In time she was recognized as a proph-
etess—a religious leader among women. She led the celebra-
tion following the debacle of the Egyptians in the Red Sea.
She is remembered in the Scriptues as a "leader" in Israel.

However, in one weak moment she disgraced herself. She,
along with Aaron, challenged the authority of Moses. "Has the
Lord indeed spoken only through Moses? Has he not spoken
through us also?" she asked.

A leader always destroys himself when he takes himself too
seriously. Miriam was jealous. The Lord has no place for
pride, envy, or jealousy. She felt she had not been properly
appreciated. Her wounded spirit sought recognition. God not
only rebuked her for her impertinence, but in the end she
owed her deliverance from leprosy to the intercession of
Moses, whom she had sought to debase.

Questions for Meditation: Do you resent it when someone else
gets more credit than you get? How far may one go to call
attention to his good deeds?

Prayer: Our Father, save us from the pangs of jealousy. Help us to
recognize every man's part in the establishment of the kingdom as
a commission from you. We pray that all your servants may be
zealous to do your work, whether they receive full recognition for
their service or not. Amen.

Monday
Hannah
1 Samuel 1:9-28

*"I have lent him to the Lord; as long as he lives, he is lent
to the Lord"* (v. 28).

Jesus told the story of the unjust judge who was hard-boiled
and feared neither God nor man, but he rendered judgment in
behalf of a widow because she refused to accept his rebuffs.
Men "ought always to pray and not lose heart" (Luke 18:1).

Hannah was such a person. For years the burden of her prayers was that she might have a son. She refused to forsake this deep desire of her heart. She promised the Lord that she would dedicate such a son to the Lord as long as he lived. Eventually God answered her prayers. True to her promise, she brought him to the house of the Lord as soon as he was weaned, that he might be trained in the Lord's service.

Every year she visited him and brought him such necessities as only a mother's heart could think to provide.

The boy became Samuel, the prophet, who judged Israel for forty years. He was not only prophet but priest and judge. Only in Moses were these three offices united in one man. Samuel was one of those very rare personalities in the Scripture about whom no evil thought or deed is recorded.

Hannah's exultation in her victory is recorded in her ecstatic song of tribute to her God:

> "There is none holy like the Lord,
>   there is none besides thee;
>   there is no rock like our God" (2:2)

Hannah's persistence in prayer paid off beyond her fondest dreams.

Questions for Meditation: What have you prayed to the Lord for most persistently? If the Lord does not grant your petition at once, do you give up?

Prayer: Our Father, give us a full measure of perseverance, not only in our petitions, but in our determination to identify ourselves with your purpose. Save us, O Lord, from following the easy, self-indulgent way. Help us to accept our role in your kingdom and play it with persistence. Amen.

Tuesday
Deborah
Judges 4:4-16

"Up! For this is the day in which the Lord has given Sisera into your hand. Does not the Lord go out before you?" (v. 14).

God commissions his leaders where he finds them. They must not only be able but willing to do his will. When the fortunes of Israel were at their lowest, he put his hand on Deborah—a wife and mother of unusual ability to inspire confidence, and endowed with rare judgment and insight.

She could have found many reasons why she should not be chosen to remedy Israel's misfortunes. She was a woman, and military leadership was essentially a man's job; she was inexperienced; she had home duties with family responsibilities; she had no army. She did not use any of these excuses. She linked duty to country with duty to God. Nations like people exist to serve God—this she believed.

She met with discouragement on every hand. Reuben was busy with his sheep and could not spare men to fight for God. Asher and Dan were engaged on the seashore with their ships. Benjamin sent advice. Issachar, Zebulun, and Naphtali sent troops. Ephraim sent token help.

On the plains of Esdraelon the battle was joined under the leadership of Barak. "Up!" commanded Deborah, "this is the day the Lord has given Sisera into your hands." God sent torrential rains. It blinded Sisera's men. It bogged his chariots down in the mud. It cut their retreat by flooding the river Kishon. "So perish all thine enemies, O Lord!" (5:31).

We need women today who will shout "Up!" when God's people should stand fast on moral issues. We need women who would rather be morally right than socially correct.

Questions for Meditation: What are some of the things you can do for the Lord today? What alibi are you using for not doing them? Do you have Deborah's faith that the Lord will be with you?

Prayer: Our Father, any man (or woman) can find excuse for not following you, but it takes a total commitment and a passion to serve you, to overcome all obstacles, and to resist the temptation to live at ease. Save us from such indifference. Let us hear your voice clearly, and grant us wisdom and willingness to respond. Amen.

Wednesday
Ruth
Ruth 1:6-18

"Entreat me not to leave you or to return from following you; for where you go I will go, and where you lodge I will lodge; your people shall be my people, and your God my God" (v. 16).

Almost all strife, conflict, and trouble between individuals and nations has its beginning in prejudice, ignorance, and selfishness. Man's customary reaction to conflict is to engage in violence, riots, and war. He has yet to learn that he is a member of the great human family, and that the well-being of one is the well-being of all.

Although Ruth was a member of an alien people and worshiped a pagan god, she sensed her identity with all humanity, and her love for Naomi, her mother-in-law, bridged the chasm of race and nationality. She could say with sincerity, "Where you go I will go, and where you lodge I will lodge; your people shall be my people, and your God my God."

She won her way into the hearts of all those she met, so that not only she but they forgot that she was an alien. Understanding humility and sincerity were the key words in her character. Around these there can be no conflict. Ruth identified herself with the human race, and the human race honored her membership. She became an ancestress of the Saviour of the world.

Questions for Meditation: How race or nationality conscious are you? Are you prepared to acknowledge yourself as a member of the human race with all the responsibility that this entails?

Prayer: Our Father, give us understanding, humility, and sincerity in all our human relationships. Forbid that we should feel superior because of race, nationality, or social status. Make us conscious of our kinship with all mankind, and make their needs our concern. Amen.

Thursday
Mary of Nazareth
Luke 1:26-35; Matthew 1:18-25

"Do not be afraid, Mary, for you have found favor with God" (Luke 1:30).

All that the Scriptures reveal about Mary, the mother of Jesus, pictures her as a devout, God-fearing woman. Every reference to her establishes her as a normal mother with inborn concern for her family. She came from a humble home, although she was a descendant of the royal Davidic line.

It is not presumptuous to assume that she was largely responsible for Jesus' early training. Although he lived in a humble carpenter's home, Jesus' remarkable knowledge of the Scriptures indicates that he had been steeped in the Scriptures at an early age—where more likely than at his mother's knee? She observed all the requirements of the Mosaic rituals. Her faith in God was such that she accepted his leadership even when she did not understand it.

Her concern for her son continued throughout his life. She experienced a mother's panic when he was missing in the big city. She was worried about the growing hostility of the religious hierarchy toward him, and she sought to bring him home into the family shelter. She followed him to Calvary, and her heart was wrenched as she watched the soldiers drive great spikes through his hands and feet. She obeyed his final instruction to "wait in Jerusalem" with the disciples, and the other followers, for the coming of the Holy Spirit.

Mary exercised no place of leadership in the early church. She played no stellar role except that she was faithful to God's plan to provide a Saviour for the world. There is no scriptural authority for her worship, or her deification. The greatest tribute to which she was entitled is the angel's statement: "You have found favor with God."

Question for Meditation: Mary's acceptance of God's role for her was direct and gracious: "Let it be to me according to your word." Are you as ready to accept God's place for you?

Prayer: Our Father, we pray that we may be faithful to accept the responsibilities you assign to us. Do not let us waver, or seek to evade your plan for our lives. May we find favor in your sight, and bless our efforts, even when they are weak and hesitating. Amen.

Friday

Mary of Magdala
Luke 8:1-3; John 20:1-18

Mary Magdalene went and said to the disciples, "I have seen the Lord"; and she told them that he had said these things to her (John 20:18).

Mary was probably a frustrated woman without purpose or goal before she met Jesus. The "seven demons" he drove out of her kept her in a constant turmoil from deep depression to high exaltation. She had material resources, but no objective for their use. She was capable of deep devotion, but without an object for her devotion.

Then she met Jesus and her whole outlook on life changed. He cured her psychotic condition. She became a stable and dependable member of the little group of women who ministered to his needs. Her wealth found an objective. She acquired a focus for all her boundless energy and enthusiasm.

She has mistakenly been identified with the "sinner" who bathed Jesus' feet with her tears and dried them with her hair (Luke 7:36-50), but there is no evidence in the record that Mary was ever unchaste. She followed Jesus over the Judean roads to Jerusalem, enraptured by his words, marveling at his miraculous deeds, and worried by the hostility of those who sought to kill him.

She stood at the cross comforting and supporting Mary, the mother of Jesus. She was the first at the tomb on resurrection morning, only to find it empty. She was the first to whom Jesus revealed himself after his resurrection, and she brought word to his disciples—"I have seen the Lord," she exulted. This was her reward for her complete dedication to the service of her master.

Questions for Meditation: Have you completely committed yourself to the Lord, or do you have some reservation? Are you saying, "I'll follow you Lord, but do not ask me to witness, or tithe, or teach a Bible class?"

Prayer: Our Father, we ask that you fill our hearts with love, our lives with purpose, our minds with understanding. May we not live aimlessly and without direction. We would commit ourselves to your service, and pray that you accept even our halting efforts because of the love that inspired them. Amen.

Saturday

Lydia

Acts 16:6-15

When she was baptized, with her household, she besought us, saying, "If you have judged me to be faithful to the Lord, come to my house and stay" (v. 15).

Paul and Silas began their second tour of preaching to the Gentiles with the idea of returning to the cities of Asia Minor, but when they arrived at Troas they were invited in a "vision" to cross over into Macedonia. Paul concluded that this was God's call to carry the gospel into Europe. This is doubtless one of the great moments in history. It was the turning point for the Christian church; it became worldwide with an open door to the west.

Arriving at Philippi, Paul searched for the customary place for prayer. In this instance it was on the riverside. There he found a group of women assembled, one of whom was Lydia. She was a businesswoman—a seller of "purple" goods from Thyratira in Asia Minor. Her clients were doubtless among the aristocrats and the wealthy, probably mostly Greeks and Romans.

The fact that she was in the group assembled for prayer speaks of her faith in the Lord. Paul had only to bring her the good news of Christ's redemption of lost sinners. "The Lord opened her heart to give heed to what was said by Paul," and she invited Paul and Silas to make her home their headquarters.

Lydia's door was the open door to Europe. How often small things lead to great and far-reaching results—both good and evil. Paul's experience emphasizes the fact that God never closes one door without opening another.

Meet the Pagans

God is the God of all peoples, all races, all nations. He controls the destiny of people even when they do not worship him. The Bible presents Israel as the special Chosen People through whom God proposes to send the Saviour, who was to redeem all peoples from their sins.

The Old Testament is the record of God's losing struggle to hold Israel's loyalty. They were continually deserting him for the pagan gods of their neighbors. To hold their loyalty he "stirred" up pagan kings to make war on Israel, only to save them from pagan bondage through the miraculous deliverance of Israel's forces. In the end he permitted pagan nations to take them into captivity in a desperate effort to regain their undivided loyalty. When they were, at last, captives in Babylon, God "stirred up" Cyrus, the Persian king, to return a loyal remnant to the homeland, that they might fulfil their mission in the world.

Thus God used pagan people, not ony to regain Israel's loyalty, but to restore its culture and religious worship.

Much of the New Testament is the record of the struggle the early followers of Christ had to see that God's plan of salvation included Gentiles as well as Jews. Here again he used Greeks and Romans to advance his purposes. Persecutions scattered his followers so that the way of salvation was proclaimed throughout the world. Gentiles were also won to the Saviour, and they contributed mightily to the dissemination of the good news everywhere. Even Gentiles like Agrippa, who would not desert his pagan gods, were used to send Paul to Rome, where he preached the gospel openly even while he was a prisoner. God's hands are not bound. He uses even his enemies to accomplish his will.

Sunday

Naaman
2 Kings 5:1-19

"I pray you, let there be given to your servant two mules' burden of earth; for henceforth your servant will not offer burnt offering or sacrifice to any god but the Lord" (v. 17).

Naaman was the foremost military man of his day, but such power and position gave him no prior standing in the kingdom of God. He was accustomed to giving orders and having them obeyed forthwith. He had yet to learn that before God he had no special privileges, but was expected to obey like the humblest soldier in his army.

It was Naaman's good fortune that he was a leper. Except for this circumstance he might never have found the Lord, since he was also a pagan. Leprosy, like sin, is no respecter of persons. To be cured of his disease, he was asked to submit his will, his pride, and his obedience to God's plan for his life. This is also the only way one can get rid of sin.

Modern leprosy is man's refusal to acknowledge a place for God in his life. We are too smart. We think our troubles can be cured through psychiatry, good deeds, tranquilizers, and relaxation. We are sick at heart; life is too much with us; we are overwhelmed with material things; we think money can buy anything; our pride tells us that we must not be "old-fashioned."

Longing to be healed is as great today as it was in Naaman's day, but a sick soul can only be healed by spiritual treatment—faith in God, obedience, and humble acknowledgment of one's sins. We must be driven to our knees before we can stand before God.

Question for Meditation: Naaman rebelled against the simple instructions Elisha gave him. He expected something difficult. Do men resist the cure for sin today because it is so simple—just believe in the Lord Jesus Christ?

Prayer: Our Father, everyone is afflicted with sin, a more deadly disease than leprosy, but you have assured us of a sure cure—faith in the Lord Jesus Christ. We pray that we may speed the day when everyone will hear the good news of your forgiveness and mercy. Let us not be weary in proclaiming this good news to a sin-sick world. Amen.

Monday
Cyrus
Ezra 1:2-8

"He is my shepherd, and he shall fulfil all my purpose" (*Isa. 44:28*).

God has a purpose for nations as well as for individuals. Cyrus was the monarch of a pagan empire, but God chose him "to subdue nations" and "to open doors." "For the sake of my servant Jacob, and Israel my chosen, I call you by your name," says the Lord. "I gird you, though you do not know me, . . . that men may know . . . that there is none besides me." (Cf. Isa. 45:1-6.)

Cyrus acknowledged God's leadership: "The Lord, the God of heaven, has given me all the kingdoms of the earth, and he has charged me to build him a house at Jerusalem" (Ezra 1:2).

God is never balked by the failure of his professed followers to do his will. When they fail him, he calls upon unbelievers. His purposes and goals must go forward. Jesus expressed this inevitable progress when he said, "I tell you, if these [his disciples] were silent, the very stones would cry out" (Luke 19:40).

There is no record that Cyrus ever forsook his pagan gods to give his undivided devotion to the Lord God Jehovah. But God called him his "shepherd" who "shall fulfil all my purpose." If America fails to fulfil God's purpose for her, we may be certain that he will find some other nation, perhaps a pagan one, to accomplish his purpose.

Questions for Meditation: Will America's apostasy compel God to "stir up" some pagan nation to save civilization? What evidence is there that America will repent?

Prayer: Our Father, make us willing and effective servants to do your will. May we not be disobedient to our understanding of your purpose in the world, and make us responsive to your call to action to build a better world. Stop our obsession with our petty, personal interests, and make us enthusiastic about the kingdom of God. Amen.

Tuesday
Rahab
Joshua 2:1-21; 6:22-25

The Lord your God is he who is God in heaven above and on earth beneath (2:11).

It pays to proclaim the power and majesty and glory of God. It pays to testify to his redeeming love. Rahab's faith in the Lord, expressed in the text for this day, was the result of the reports of God's leadership of Israel which came to her attention. "We have heard," she said, recounting the reports of God's power.

The proclamation of God's presence in Israel's camp did three things: (1) It won Rahab's active assistance to Israel's entry into the Promised Land. She provided Joshua's spies with important information. (2) It saved the lives of the spies, and assured the safety of her own family. (3) It produced in her a faith in God, and at the risk of her life she committed herself to Israel's God. According to Matthew 1:5 she became the mother of Boaz, the great-grandfather of David, and so an ancestress of the Saviour of the world.

No one can forsee where a sincere testimony for God may lead, nor the cost to the kingdom of God when such a testimony is withheld. Before her encounter with God, Rahab was hardly a virtuous woman, but through God's mercy and grace she became a "new creation" and served the Lord faithfully. No one can sink so low that God's grace cannot redeem and re-create the fallen.

Question for Meditation: Why did God choose to work through a questionable character like Rahab to accomplish his purpose?

Prayer: Our Father, who can understand your ways and foresee how you can take our small efforts and make them significant in the progress of your kingdom. Give us a faith that will drive us to do our best for you and to trust you for the blessing that only you can give. Amen.

Makeda (Queen of Sheba)
1 Kings 10:1-13

King Solomon gave to the queen of Sheba all that she desired. . . . So she turned and went back to her own land (v. 13).

The queen was lured to Jerusalem by the fame of King Solomon. She came on a sight-seeing holiday. She came to see for herself the greatness and wisdom of Solomon, and the record says the king answered all her questions and there was nothing hidden that the king did not explain to her. She was overwhelmed by Solomon's greatness and "the house [Temple] that he had built." And when the queen had seen all—"and his burnt offerings which he offered at the house of the Lord," she was overcome with admiration and said, "Blessed be the Lord your God, who has delighted in you and set you on the throne of Israel!"

There is no record that the queen was interested in Solomon's faith in the Lord, nor that Solomon attributed any of his greatness and wisdom to the Lord. The Temple aroused her admiration as an exquisite piece of architecture. She witnessed a sacrifice in the Temple but it did not excite her interest in its significance. Solomon is said to have told her everything. Did he tell her that the greatness of the Lord God Jehovah is far more important than his own greatness? Did he tell her that the Lord is one God and there is none other?

Men and women throughout the ages have been wont to praise God as an institution, a tradition, a superstition, or a philosophical idea. They built shrines to his name; they engaged in elaborate rituals; they offered prayers and sang songs of praise; but they did not enthrone him in their lives; they did not make him the Lord of their lives.

To the queen of Sheba the Temple was only a magnificent spectacle. The episode closes with the queen's acceptance of Solomon's gifts, and she turned and went back to her own land—without the Lord in her heart.

Questions for Meditation: Did Solomon miss an opportunity to lead the queen to faith in his God? Or, perhaps, Solomon's own faith was not that strong. What would you have done?

Prayer: Our Father, all people in all lands have need to know you —the only God—the Creator, the Saviour, the Judge of the world. May we lose no opportunity to proclaim your grace and mercy for all mankind. Amen.

Thursday
Agrippa
Acts 25:13 to 26:29

Then Agrippa said unto Paul, Almost thou persuadest me to be a Christian (26:28, KJV).

Almost is not good enough. The road to eternal death is strewn with "almosts." Where are the people who "almost" put their faith in the Lord; who have "almost" committed their lives to do the will of God; who have "almost" asked God to forgive their sins; who have "almost" become disciples of Christ?

> "Almost" cannot avail;
> "Almost" is but to fail!
> Sad, sad but bitter wail—
> "Almost," but lost!
> PHILIP P. BLISS

There is no record that Agrippa ever went all the way. He was nearer the kingdom of God that day than he would ever be again. There is no such person as a half persuaded Christian.

Many people listen to the proclamation of God's mercy and grace; they listen with sympathetic approval; they are tempted to respond; their hearts and minds acknowledge the validity of the appeal, but they do not make the commitment. They reject the Lord by doing nothing.

Agrippa's pagan gods did not make the demands upon his life that Christ makes. He sold the "abundant life" which Christ promised his followers for a mess of pottage.

"Almost," but lost.

Questions for Meditation: Why do so many come so close to accepting the salvation for which Christ died—and then don't? Is Satan's appeal stronger than the Lord's?

Prayer: Our Father, make us ready to go all the way in our rejection of sin and all its associations. Give us an ear trained to hear your voice as it speaks to us about the things that make our lives more abundantly useful. Give us the will to obey. Amen.

Friday
The Centurion in Capernaum
Luke 7:1-10

When Jesus heard this he marveled at him, and turned and said to the multitude that followed him, "I tell you, not even in Israel have I found such faith" (v. 9).

How appropriate that Jesus should find this superlative example of faith in a pagan—a Roman soldier. But how sad that of all God's chosen people who had centuries of exposure to God's leadership and blessings, not one could match this pagan soldier's faith.

Our birth in a Christian land, our living in a Christian

home, our attendance at God's services of worship do not give us any prior claim on Jesus' approval. Rather, these privileges add to our responsibility for a fruitful spiritual product. "Not every one who says to me, 'Lord, Lord,' shall enter the kingdom of heaven, but he who does the will of my Father who is in heaven" (Matt. 7:21).

The centurion had a practical approach to Jesus' power. He compared it to his own power over those who were subservient to him. He had faith to believe that Jesus could command the forces of nature as effectively as he commanded his men. Nor was he displaying any arrogance or pride to bring Jesus to the bedside of his servant. Rather, it was his sincere humility which made him feel unworthy to have Jesus come under his roof that prompted the display of his superlative faith. "I am not worthy," he said. This is still a basic attitude for repentant sinners. It is by God's grace, not our merit, that we are saved.

Questions for Meditation: What prompted the centurion's faith in Jesus? Did he see Jesus at work? Did someone tell him about it? How much evidence must you have to acquire such faith?

Prayer: Our Father, our faith in you is so wavering and at times uncertain that we cannot be effective witnesses. Like the father who came to Jesus to cure his son we must say: "Help our unbelief." Give us a faith that will enable us, with your help, to transform our dreams into deeds, our hopes for a better world into reality. Amen.

The Town Clerk

Acts 19:23-30

*When the town clerk had quieted the crowd, he said, . . .
"You have brought these men here who are neither sacri-
legious nor blasphemers of our goddess. If therefore Demetrius and the craftsmen with him have a complaint against
any one, the courts are open" (vv. 35-38).*

When people resort to riots and violence they thereby admit
that they are espousing an irrational cause. In a society gov-
erned by laws, and not by men, any worthy cause can find its
most dependable support in its reliance upon the processes of
the law. So the town clerk rightly tells Demetrius, the plain-
tiff, that the "courts are open," and warns the rioters that there
is "no cause that we can give to justify this commotion."

It took courage and prestige for the town clerk (mayor?) to
face the mob and subdue it with the voice of reason. Two
years of work by Paul was at stake in this rebellion, stirred up
by a man who had a vested interest in the local pagan
religion.

Demetrius is the prototype of the businessman who is never
as pious as when the defense of religion is good for his
business. "There is danger," said he, "not only that this trade
of ours may come into disrepute but also that the temple of
the great goddess Artemis may count for nothing." Note, the
worry about the goddess was an afterthought.

The marks of a conscientious public official is his readiness
to support the process of law and order at whatever cost to his
own safety or political future. Any man is engaged in a sorry
pursuit when he participates or is engaged in a lawless course
of action.

Meet the Fictional Characters

All the fictional characters in the Bible are nameless. Only Job may be an exception. Almost all the fictional characters in the New Testament are in the four Gospels, and in each instance they are characters in stories Jesus told to illustrate his teaching.

No doubt many of Jesus' stories relate to incidents Jesus witnessed as a boy or young man around his home neighborhood in Nazareth. Tales like that of the unjust judge, the prodigal son, and the rich farmer might have made a headline in the local newspaper. Some of the scenes must have excited the interest of a small boy, like the woman who scoured her home to find a coin that had rolled under the sofa, or the shepherd's all-night search for the sheep that went astray. Doubtless he was impressed with the tiny seed that grew into a mighty tree, or the seed that fell along the way for the birds to pick up.

Jesus was a matchless storyteller. His famous discourses were studded with homely pictures: "Consider the lilies of the field"; "Nor do men light a lamp and put it under a bushel"; "If salt has lost its taste, how shall its saltness be restored? It is fit neither for the land nor for the dunghill"; "Look at the birds of the air: . . . your heavenly Father feeds them." All these describe an alert boy who noticed the little things that filled his day, and later he used them to enliven his teaching.

Needless to say, Jesus' storytelling was not directed toward entertainment, but each story illustrated his teaching graphically. How better could he dramatize God's boundless love for his erring children than the picture of a waiting father who refused to give up hope that his prodigal son would return, and who saw and recognized him while he was still afar off.

Sunday

The Prodigal Son
Luke 15:11-24

But when he came to himself he said, . . . "Father, I have sinned against heaven and before you" (*vv. 17-18*).

The story of the prodigal son is preceded by the stories of the lost sheep and the lost coin. Together these stories were told to emphasize God's unlimited concern for those who are lost.

The conditions under which the prodigal son found himself were the inevitable results of his own obsession. He was not a "bad boy." Like many boys before him, and after him, he was intent on being "on his own." The restrictions of a circumspect home were too much for him. He would spread his wings. He would see the world. He would not be confined by the morality of a waning generation. He wanted to be free to live his own life without the oversight of a father who, he thought, did not understand him.

He made three miscalculations. First, he did not understand that the moral and social conventions against which he rebelled were not whims of an insensitive and arbitrary father, but they were the bulwarks of an orderly society hammered out through countless generations, and they represented the accumulated wisdom of the human race. To ignore this basic human experience could only lead to disaster—and it did.

Second, he trusted in his possessions. Money, he found, attracted "friends"—of a kind. While his money lasted he was the toast of the town. But when his money was gone, he learned how ephemeral his popularity was. "And no one gave him anything" (v. 16).

Third, he misjudged his father. He was not the stubborn, intolerant reactionary he thought. He was a compassionate and forgiving father, yearning for the return of his wayward son.

God is like that, Jesus was saying. Regardless of how far his children wander away, he is ever ready, waiting for the prodigal to come home. "While he [is] yet at a distance" God meets him with compassion and forgiveness, "for this my son was dead, and is alive again."

Questions for Meditation: What was the turning point in this young man's rebellion? What qualified him for return to his place in the family?

Prayer: Our Father, we are overwhelmed by your persistent and matchless love for all your children. We would be worthy of the love of our Lord, Jesus Christ, who went to the cross for us. Grant that we may "come to ourselves" and turn our steps homeward and to you. Amen.

Monday

The Elder Brother

Luke 15:25-32

But he was angry and refused to go in (v. 28).

Respectability frequently hides an evil and unforgiving heart.

The only consolation the father of this story had during the years when he was grieving for the loss of his wayward son, was the presence of his steady older brother. Here was a man, dependable and trustworthy, who never gave his father a moment's anxiety or worry. He attended strictly to his responsibilities. He was solid and practical. He was content with his station in life. He was not demanding or critical. He stood well in the community. He was a deacon in his church. People loved to hear him pray in public. They would contrast him approvingly with his prodigal brother, about whose escapades in the city they heard from time to time.

The father leaned heavily upon him. Since the younger son had taken his share of the family fortune, the old homestead was the sole inheritance of the elder brother. He was assured that someday he would come into his own and take his place as one of the respected older citizens of the community.

But underneath this placid and respected exterior there was a rebellious and vindictive heart. How he envied his brother's independence, and how he hated him. Every report of his brother's profligate experience filled him with jealousy and anger. When the news of his brother's crash reached him, he was glad.

No wonder he refused to join in the festivities arranged for the return of the penitent, contrite, and humbled brother. All the pent-up emotions of the years came to the surface. He could find nothing in his heart about which to rejoice. "He was angry and refused to go in" (v. 28).

"Man looks on the outward appearance, but the Lord looks on the heart" (1 Sam. 16:7).

Question for Meditation: Which of the two boys would you say was the most desirable son?

Prayer: Our Father, purify our hearts of all malice, jealousy, and self-righteousness. Forbid that we should exult over the wayward-ness of our brothers and rejoice at their misfortunes—even when such misfortunes are self-inflicted. Give us a compassionate heart that seeks the well-being of all people—even the unlovely ones. Amen.

Tuesday
The Rich Farmer
Luke 12:15-20

"A man's life does not consist in the abundance of his pos-sessions" (v. 15).

Possessions and life are not the same thing, nor is a man's life a part of his possessions. However rich a man may be, his life is not his own. Job reminds us that "the Lord gave, and the Lord has taken away" (1:21).

There is no indication that the farmer ever credited any of his wealth to God. He refused to recognize that even such blessings as rain and sunshine had any part in the develop-ment of his bumper crops. Note his egotistical boast: "my barns," "my grain," "my goods," "my soul." The writer of Deuteronomy warns: "Beware lest you say in your heart, 'My power and the might of my hand have gotten me this wealth.' You shall remember the Lord your God, for it is he who gives you power to get wealth" (8:17-18).

Wealth always creates a problem, whether its owner real-izes it or not. What to do with it? That's the problem. The farmer had the answer to that question too. "Take your ease," he said, "eat, drink, be merry." How many regard this as the height of "living." But intemperance is not synonymous with abundant living. Moreover, he was mistaken when he assumed that wealth and long life went together—"goods laid up for many years," he boasted.

Up to this time the farmer did all the talking, but God always has the last word. "Fool!" God said. End of a misdirected life!

The farmer's sin was the sin of uselessness. With all his wealth he thought of nothing except his own gratification. "But seek first his kingdom and his righteousness, and all these things shall be yours as well" was Jesus' formula for abundant living.

Questions for Meditation: How much credit do you honestly think you deserve for the material things you enjoy? How much is God's? To what extent are you entitled to use it for yourself?

Prayer: Our Father, we acknowledge our dependence upon you not only for our spiritual blessings, but for our material blessings too. All that we have comes from you, and we are your designated stewards. Grant that we may use it for the coming of your kingdom among men and not just for our comfort and pleasure. Amen.

Wednesday
The Rich Man
Luke 16:19-31

"There was a rich man, who was clothed in purple and fine linen and who feasted sumptuously every day" (v. 19).

This is all we are told about this man's life. He was absorbed in the business of gratifying his physical appetites. He was oblivious to the needs of people around him. He would not share his wealth lest there be not enough left to satisfy his desires. His entire life was built around his material security. As a businessman he worried about investments, taxes, business cycles, cost of living, sales, inflation, depressions, old age, and ill health. But never about his soul!

Then suddenly the scene changes; his wealth has no value whatever in his new environment. All the things he thought were important have vanished. For the first time he became aware of needs which his wealth could not satisfy. He realized that he had missed the whole purpose of life—preparation to face God.

In his torment he became envious of those who were serene and calm, who had an abiding faith that God is in control of the universe, who did not go to pieces when banks closed and stock markets crashed, who faced death like they always faced life—unafraid, who believed in the goodness of God and the integrity of their neighbors, who had used their wealth to lay up treasures in heaven.

In his doomed condition he had one redeeming impulse. He prayed for his brothers—but it was too late. "We must work the works of him who sent me, while it is day; night comes, when no one can work" (John 9:4).

Questions for Meditation: How many people come to the end of their lives only to find that they missed its real purpose? What is life's real purpose?

Prayer: Our Father, remind us daily that the purpose of life is to prepare ourselves to live in fellowship with you both here and hereafter. May we reject all temptations to live for ourselves. May we dedicate to you, not only our material possessions, but our hearts and lives as well. Amen.

Thursday

The Good Samaritan

Luke 10:30-37

A Samaritan, as he journeyed, came to where he was; and when he saw him, he had compassion (v. 33).

When Jesus wanted to illustrate, in a story, the kind of people who would qualify in the role of neighborliness, he selected, of all people, a Samaritan. To the Jews the Samaritans were their most despised and detested neighbors. Because Samaria lay between Galilee and the Jerusalem area, a devout Jew would cross the Jordan River and go miles out of his way through Perea in order to avoid Samaritan soil.

When Jesus planned his last visit to Jerusalem, he deliberately chose to go through Samaria. But the disciples who went ahead to prepare for the arrival of Jesus' party were repulsed by the Samaritans. The humiliated disciples wanted to "bid fire come down from heaven and consume them" (9:54). But Jesus rebuked them and they went on to another village.

It was on the heels of this rebuff that Jesus chose to tell this story of the good Samaritan, who went out of his way to show kindness and helpfulness to the victim of a highway robbery. It was as if Jesus was eager to say that Samaritans are children of God too; that they respond to human need with all compassion and love; that no people, as a people, can be classed as evil or iniquitous; that all men must be judged on their personal merits, and that doing good deserves to be recognized wherever it is found.

The "good Samaritan" has become a universal symbol of neighborly concern whom we are charged to emulate—"Go and do likewise," said Jesus.

Questions for Meditation: When Jesus said you shall love your neighbor as yourself, what did he mean? How do you love yourself?

Prayer: Our Father, we are so inclined to look down on people of another race or another country or religious faith, that we erect barriers between us. We do not take time from our personal pursuits to show compassion for those less fortunate than ourselves. Lord, have mercy on us and forgive us. Amen.

Friday
The Tax Collector at Prayer
Luke 18:9-14

"God, be merciful to me a sinner!" (*v. 13*).

The Pharisee was doubtless a good man. Look at him. Can anyone match him for his piety? But he was not really praying. He was admiring himself. He was afraid God would overlook his many beautiful virtues. The fact that he addressed God did not mean that God paid attention to his petition. His attitude was one of snobbishness—and God hates snobbishness. He is never reached through hypocritical prayers.

God was surely touched by the humble prayer of the publican. There was no ostentation, no pride, no boasting—just a simple plea for mercy, and an acknowledgment of sin. These are the basic ingredients of an effective prayer.

It was not only the content of the prayer that was significant. The record says he "would not even lift up his eyes to heaven." Here was dramatic recognition of the power and the majesty of God. To him it was a very great privilege to be able to address God and make his heart's desire known. He did not abuse the privilege by much vain talk. In seven simple words he made his most personal needs known.

The ether waves are filled with music and voices. We can listen in on this unseen world through that delicate instrument we call the radio. So prayer is the delicate instrument through which we join the spiritual forces of the universe. When we pray, we are at one with all others who are in communion with the Father. To effect such communication we must be on the same "wave length" with the Lord. "The prayer of a righteous man has great power in its effects" (James 5:16).

Questions for Meditation: When you pray, "Forgive us our debts, as we also have forgiven our debtors," have you really forgiven your debtors—all of them?—even those that gossiped about you and lied to you?

Prayer: Our Father, like the publican we are in need of your mercy and forgiveness. We, too, acknowledge our sins. Do not hold them against us. Before we ask your forgiveness, we have forgiven all those who have wronged us. May we be so occupied in your service that sin and evil will find no place in our lives. Amen.

Saturday

The Priest and the Levite
Luke 10:30-37

When he saw him he passed by on the other side (v. 31).

The lack of human compassion is a blot on the character of any man, but when human suffering fails to awaken a responsive chord in the hearts of Christians, it is time to question the sincerity of their spiritual profession.

The priest and the Levite were acknowledged leaders of the religious community of their day. Doubtless they were on their way to perform some significant religious service. The priest was probably on his way to conduct a service at the synagogue in Jericho, and he was late. The Levite was scheduled to be in Jerusalem to prepare the altar for the people who would be coming to offer their sacrifices. He, too, was pressed for time.

Both of these men had, in their view, acceptable excuses not to be diverted from their religious missions by helping the unfortunate man in the ditch by the wayside. They were good men, honored by their people with important duties. They suffered Jesus' rebuke in the story, not because they were wicked or morally bad, but because they showed no compassion, and did nothing. Compassion for human need is equivalent to service to God—"As you did it to one of the least of these my brethren, you did it to me" (Matt. 25:40).

To be acceptable before the Lord requires more than pious prayers, reading the Scriptures, going to church, paying the tithe, or singing a hymn. Jesus said it means to take up one's cross and follow him.

Questions for Meditation: When did you last shrug off an opportunity to help someone in need, because you were too busy? Do you feel comfortable when you pass the responsibility to the United Charities?

Prayer: Our Father, may we never be so busy that we disregard the needs of people around us. Make us compassionate and generous toward everyone in need, especially those who are outside our circle of personal friends. May we redraw the circle and include them in it. Amen.

Twelfth Week
Meet the
Inquirers

There are only two kinds of people who never ask questions. One is the fellow who knows everything. He has all the answers; he does not need to ask questions (so he thinks). The other is the stupid fellow who does not know enough to ask questions. Between these two extremes are all the honest seekers after truth. The depth of the questions they ask is determined by their interest in and their insight into the truth.

As might be expected, the most penetrating and deepest questions in all literature are contained in the Bible: questions which have perplexed the most astute scholars of the world; questions which were asked out of the depths of despair; questions asked for light and guidance in life's critical situations; questions of incredulity and amazement.

These questions are not always answered immediately and categorically. God is not a schoolteacher with a textbook and a slide rule. He has endowed people with intelligence and discernment. By exposing them to truth and reality he expects them to find the answers to their own questions. When the answers are not immediately discernible, we live by faith until they are.

This week's study includes seven questions that mankind has faced through many generations.

Sunday
Job
Job 3:1-26

"Why did I not die at birth?" (v. 11).

Job had reached the bottomless pit of despair and hopelessness, his lament occasioned by the multitude of his misfortunes, sounds the depths of human misery. Even his wife, looking upon his misery, advised him to "Curse God, and die" (2:9).

But Job was made of sterner stuff. He refused to desert God because of his misfortunes. "The Lord gave, and the Lord has taken away; blessed be the name of the Lord," he said. Even when the plagues attacked him personally with "loathsome sores," he would not repudiate God. "Shall we [not] receive good [things] at the hand of God, and shall we not receive evil?" Take the bad with the good was Job's philosophy.

Job had no idea how badly off he really was until his friends convinced him. Seven days of uninterrupted weeping and emotional eruption would result in despair and hopelessness in the most sanguine personality. This plunged him into his deepest despair. "Why did I not die at birth?" he asked.

With this question Job raised a question millions have asked: Why do good men suffer? If God is omnipotent and permits the innocent to suffer, he cannot be a just God, Job's friends reasoned. But if God exercised his omnipotence to save men from suffering, he makes puppets of them, and that defeats the purpose he had in mind when he created man in his own image.

It was not God who sent Job's adversities. It was Satan. But God uses man's adversities to make him more Godlike. For this man must trust him even when he does not understand. Eventually Job could say: "I had heard of thee by the hearing of the ear, but now my eye sees thee." Many people know about God from what others have told them, but no one really knows God until he "sees" him personally. Adversity did this for Job.

God's supreme purpose is to make men worthy to be his creation. "Gird up your loins like a man," God says. "Deck yourself with majesty and dignity; clothe yourself with glory," for you are God's handiwork.

In the end Job confesses, "I have uttered what I did not understand," and when he prayed for his friends, the Lord restored his fortune. Adversity drove him back to the source of his faith.

Questions for Meditation: What do you do with adversity? Is it your opportunity to prove and strengthen your faith? Or do you curse God?

Prayer: Our Father, when misfortunes and adversity overwhelm us, we pray that we may recognize them as opportunities to prove our faith in you. Do not let them destroy our faith. Grant that because of them we may see you more clearly and trust you more securely. Amen.

Monday
David
Psalm 22:1-8; 19-21

My God, my God, why hast thou forsaken me? (v. 1).

With all of David's greatness he was an intensely human man. He succumbed to one of the oldest sins of the human race; he prayed the Lord for the destruction of his enemies; in spite of the Lord's goodness to him, he was prone to believe that he had been forsaken and he charged the Lord with desertion. When David cried, "My God, my God, why hast thou forsaken me?" he was voicing the cry of many before and after him. When God does not respond quickly to our petitions, his very existence, and certainly his concern for us, becomes suspect. It is as if God should be standing at our door ready to grant our slightest wish. With how much better reason could God ask us: "Why have you forsaken me?"

To be forsaken by God is a calamity of the first order. But such a catastrophe is never initiated by the Lord. The Scriptures are filled with God's repudiation of his people, but only after *they* had repudiated him. How often do men charge God with desertion, especially from beds of affliction or loss of loved ones, when they have ignored him, even scorned him, for years.

Tuesday
Paul
Acts 22:3-11

"What shall I do, Lord?" (v. 10).

Paul's sincere desire to serve the Lord, even during the years when he was persecuting the early church, can never be questioned. He believed that Jesus had been condemned justly for blasphemy and resistance to the established order. He believed that Jesus' condemnation to the cross was God's disapproval of an unholy life. He was convinced, therefore, that his persecution of Jesus' followers, who were persistently perpetuating the influence of Jesus and his teaching, was what God wanted him to do.

When he was confronted by Jesus on the road to Damascus, therefore, he was genuinely bewildered. His whole world was about to cave in on him. He first assured himself about the identity of his challenger: "Who are you?" When he was satisfied that the Lord himself was confronting him, he was ready to listen: "What shall I do, Lord?"

Question for Meditation: How often is a prayer for God's guidance on your lips?

Prayer: Our Father, show us what you would have us do. Make us alert to your voice and obedient to your commands. Amen.

Wednesday
Nathanael
John 1:45-51

"How do you know me?" (v. 48).

Nathanael was obviously a provincial, steeped in local prejudice. Although he was himself a Galilean from Cana, he could see nothing good come out of neighboring Nazareth. When Philip told him about the new prophet, he sneered at the likelihood of anyone of importance coming from such a town. But Philip would not be drawn into a controversy about the merits of Galilean towns. He closed the conversation with a simple, "Come and see" [for yourself].

When Nathanael was introduced to Jesus, his little provincial world collapsed. One look into the face of Jesus and a new dimension was added to his little world. In that face he saw mirrored the whole human race. There was infinite compassion, love, and mercy for all mankind. When Jesus, with deft insight, commended him for his forthrightness and sincerity, he could only blurt out: "How do you know me?"

Prayer: Our Father, remind us day by day that you see us—at our best and at our worst. You know every inclination of our heart. You do not approve our weaknesses and our waywardness, but you assure us strength to meet every temptation. Amen.

Thursday
The Young Lawyer
Mark 12:28-34

"Which commandment is the first of all? (v. 28).

In asking this question this young man was not seriously seeking light and information. He was trying to trap Jesus. Argument about the importance of the laws was a hot-stove pastime of Jewish intellectuals. They could spend long hours debating the primacy of various laws. It gave them a feeling of piety to be so engaged, without at the same time evoking more serious obligations to obey the laws. They were like people today who engage in spirited argument about their favorite religious doctrine, supported, of course, by their own interpretation of the Scriptures.

Jesus answered the lawyer's question by quoting the first of the Ten Commandments. In doing so he aligned himself with Moses, about whose authority none of the various legal cliques had the temerity to differ. But Jesus went beyond the question asked and brought obedience to God's Commandment down to human relationships. "The second," he said, "is this, "You shall love your neighbor as yourself." On what better principle can human society be built?

Friday
Pilate
Matthew 27:15-23

"Then what shall I do with Jesus who is called Christ?"
(v. 22).

Pilate surrendered to the mob when he asked them to pass sentence on Jesus. When has justice ever been decreed by a mob? Pilate was a weak and ineffective magistrate. He held his job through political influence, not by reason of his ability to deal with an intransigent people.

The record plainly states that he knew Jesus was indicted by the Jews because of malicious motives, and that the charge of treason to Caesar was without foundation. In fact, he did not call for a single witness to be brought before him to testify to the charge. The absence of such evidence, in itself, was sufficient grounds to release Jesus. Torn between pleasing the mob and doing his duty, Pilate chose the easy way. To have the Jews in his debt could be very helpful to him politically.

But Pilate's question has a much deeper significance than he could possibly foresee. "What shall I do with Jesus?" is a question every person who has been exposed to the gospel and God's magnanimous gift of grace to lost sinners must answer. Some will ignore it—that means rejection. Some will vacillate between doing what their consciences and good judgment tells them they ought to do. Some will procrastinate —put it off. These are all rejections.

"Today, when you hear his voice, do not harden your hearts" (Heb. 4:7).

Questions for Meditation: Someone has said that Pilate asked the most important question anyone can ask. Can you think of one more important? How do you answer it?

Saturday
The Philippian Jailer
Acts 16:20-34

"What must I do to be saved?" (v. 30).

Redemption through faith in the Lord Jesus involves more than a resolve to "do better." It is not a reformation, although redemption always results in reformation. Redemption is a revolution. It means a "new birth"—a spiritual birth. Paul says: "If any one is in Christ, he is a new creation" (2 Cor. 5:17).

The jailer accepted Paul's answer: "Believe in the Lord Jesus" (v. 31). He did not understand the process of spiritual birth, but he acted on the light he had. He saw himself as alienated from God, and he recognized that Paul and Silas who could sing in prison had something he longed to have.

As a result of his faith he became a "new creation." He had a new viewpoint. He was no longer a hard-boiled jailer, but a brother in Christ with Paul and Silas. His first act as a new creation was to lead his family to Christ.

What happens when redeemed men become new creations? The weak, vacillating Peter became a flaming evangel. The conniving Zacchaeus not only became an honest tax collector, but he made restitution for the wrong he had committed. The Samaritan woman of Sychar brought a whole town to Jesus. The misguided Saul became Paul the great bearer of good news to all people.

Prayer: Our Father, you have made "new creations" out of everyone who puts his faith in you. Implant in each of us a new spirit, a new passion for serving you, a new relationship with our fellowman. Amen.